NOT A SUICIDE PACT

Not a Suicide Pact

. . .

THE CONSTITUTION IN A

TIME OF NATIONAL EMERGENCY

Richard A. Posner

OXFORD
UNIVERSITY PRESS

2006

OXFORD
UNIVERSITY PRESS

Oxford University Press, Inc., publishes works that further
Oxford University's objective of excellence
in research, scholarship, and education.

Oxford   New York
Auckland   Cape Town   Dar es Salaam   Hong Kong   Karachi
Kuala Lumpur   Madrid   Melbourne   Mexico City   Nairobi
New Delhi   Shanghai   Taipei   Toronto

With offices in
Argentina   Austria   Brazil   Chile   Czech Republic   France   Greece
Guatemala   Hungary   Italy   Japan   Poland   Portugal   Singapore
South Korea   Switzerland   Thailand   Turkey   Ukraine   Vietnam

Copyright © 2006 by Oxford University Press

Published by Oxford University Press, Inc.
198 Madison Avenue, New York, New York 10016
www.oup.com

Library of Congress Cataloging-in-Publication Data
Posner, Richard A.
Not a suicide pact : the constitution in a time
of national emergency / by Richard A. Posner.
p. cm.   Includes index.
ISBN-13: 978-0-19-530427-5 (cloth)

1. Civil rights—United States.
2. National security—Law and legislation—United States.
I. Title.
KF4749.P67 2006   342.7308'5—dc22
2006005345

Printed in the United States of America
on acid-free paper

The choice is not between order and liberty. It is between liberty with order and anarchy without either. There is danger that, if the Court does not temper its doctrinaire logic with a little practical wisdom, it will convert the constitutional Bill of Rights into a suicide pact.

—JUSTICE ROBERT JACKSON,
DISSENTING IN *TERMINIELLO V. CITY OF CHICAGO* (1949)

. . .

While the Constitution protects against invasions of individual rights, it is not a suicide pact.

—JUSTICE ARTHUR GOLDBERG,
FOR THE COURT, IN *KENNEDY V. MENDOZA-MARTINEZ* (1963)

. . .

As Justice Jackson put it in a now often-quoted remark, we cannot allow our Constitution and our shared sense of decency to become a suicide pact.

—PROFESSOR RONALD DWORKIN,
IN THE *NEW YORK REVIEW OF BOOKS* (2002)

Contents

CONTENTS

. . .

Editors' Note

We hold these truths to be self-evident, that all men are created
equal, that they are endowed by their Creator with certain unalien-
able Rights. . . .

—THE DECLARATION OF INDEPENDENCE

This volume is the first in a new series on Inalienable Rights. Each
book illuminates why a right or set of rights is in the Constitution (or
has remained outside it), and then explores the controversies the
right has provoked. Rights invite discussion: What is a constitutional
right? What are the counterbalancing duties? Rights are often inde-
terminate and under pressure from a variety of sources. Authors in
this series have their own points of view, and in these volumes they
will declare and defend them. Civic debate is at the heart of the
American political process. The Inalienable Rights series is designed
to challenge readers to question their own assumptions about these
foundational canons of our society.

Richard Posner's *Not a Suicide Pact: The Constitution in a Time of National Emergency* addresses a key dilemma as we struggle to maintain

our equilibrium in an era of intense security concerns and growing threats to long-held liberties. When terrorists can kill tens of thousands by spraying aerosolized anthrax or detonating dirty bombs, how should we properly balance our interest in personal liberty with our interest in public safety? What are the roles of the executive, the Congress, and the judiciary when a crisis is at hand? To what extent should civil liberties vary with threat levels?

Richard Posner here dissects the constitutional issues raised by such controversial policies as detention, torture, data mining, and the interception of phone calls and other electronic communications. He argues that rights should be modified according to circumstance and that we must find a *pragmatic* balance between personal liberty and community safety. Such balancing cannot easily be translated into fixed rules, or even legislation. Sometimes, as with Lincoln's decision to suspend habeas corpus during the Civil War, the immediate situation must take precedence over rules. Posner contends that if we do not allow the Constitution to bend, it may break.

This is a controversial claim, and it is therefore in the spirit of this series. In a vibrant democracy, controversial viewpoints stimulate critical engagement. The framers of the Constitution could not have envisioned the cell phone, the wiretap, or the dirty bomb, but they were not naïve about societal and technological change. They hoped that the democratic processes they had created would enable enlightened citizens and their representatives to amend or adapt traditional policies as necessary after suitable debate.

The Bill of Rights itself was controversial and almost died in Congress. James Madison championed the idea of enumerating specific freedoms in the new Constitution by arguing that only by securing "the great rights of mankind" could abuse of power be prevented. Madison maintained that the courts, the "independent tribunals of justice," would make themselves "the guardian of those rights" and serve as "an impenetrable bulwark" against improper "assumption of power in the legislative or executive." Which leads us back to Richard Posner's thesis. Are the courts the primary guardians of our rights, or must they defer to the executive "in time of national emergency"? Who is best positioned to make the pragmatic judgments on which our safety and liberties depend? Let the debate begin.

April 2006   Geoffrey R. Stone
                                                      Dedi Felman

NOT A SUICIDE PACT

. . .

Introduction

THIS IS A BOOK ABOUT THE CONSTITUTIONAL RIGHTS that impinge on the measures for the protection of national security that the U.S. government has taken in response to the terrorist attacks of September 11, 2001. It is thus about the marginal adjustments in such rights that practical-minded judges make when the values that underlie the rights—values such as personal liberty and privacy—come into conflict with values of equal importance, such as public safety, suddenly magnified by the onset of a national emergency. Like any brittle thing, a Constitution that will not bend will break.

The history of the United States has been punctuated by these emergencies. The greatest, after the early years of the Republic, was the Civil War; the crisis of constitutionalism that emergencies beget remains a legacy of that desperate struggle. The number of national emergencies accelerated in the twentieth century as the United States became a world power and then a nuclear power confronting other nuclear powers. There were the two world wars; the nation's greatest economic depression, coinciding with the rise of totalitarianism abroad in the 1930s; the Cold War, which lasted from 1948 to

1989 and was punctuated by episodes of espionage, war, and near war (for example, the Cuban missile crisis); and, embedded within the Cold War, the Vietnam War and the domestic unrest and governmental overreactions that the war sparked in the late 1960s and early 1970s. All these episodes placed pressure on existing constitutional understandings. Now, in the early years of the twenty-first century, the nation faces the intertwined menaces of global terrorism and proliferation of weapons of mass destruction. A city can be destroyed by an atomic bomb the size of a melon, which if coated with lead would be undetectable. Large stretches of a city can be rendered uninhabitable, perhaps for decades, merely by the explosion of a conventional bomb that has been coated with radioactive material. Smallpox virus bioengineered to make it even more toxic and vaccines ineffectual, then aerosolized and sprayed in a major airport, might kill millions of people. Our terrorist enemies have the will to do such things and abundant opportunities, because our borders are porous both to enemies and to containers. They will soon have the means as well. The march of technology has increased the variety and lethality of weapons of mass destruction, especially the biological, and also, critically, their accessibility. Aided by the disintegration of the Soviet Union and the acquisition of nuclear weapons by unstable nations (Pakistan and North Korea, soon to be joined, in all likelihood, by Iran), technological progress is making weapons of mass destruction ever more accessible both to terrorist groups (and even individuals) and to hostile nations that are not major powers. The problem of proliferation is more serious today than it was in what now seem the almost halcyon days of the Cold War; it will be even more serious tomorrow.

I am not a Chicken Little, and I agree with those who argue that our vigorous campaign against al-Qaeda and our extensive if chaotic efforts at improving homeland security have bought us a breathing space against terrorist attacks on U.S. territory. But how long will this breathing space last? The terrorists, their leadership decimated and dispersed, may be reeling, but they have not been defeated. In January 2006 Osama bin Laden declared that there would be further terrorist attacks on the United States; it would be reckless to dismiss his declaration as idle boasting. This is not the time to let down our guard.

David Luban asks: "What sacrifice in our rights would we be willing to undergo to reduce the already-small probability of another September 11 by a factor of, say, one in ten? From, let us say, one percent annually to point-nine percent—an annual saving of less than half a statistical life?" Those are not good questions. We have no idea whether the probability of another 9/11 (or worse) is only 1 percent.

The research that I have been conducting for the past several years on catastrophic risks, international terrorism, and national security intelligence has persuaded me that we live in a time of grave and increasing danger, comparable to what the nation faced at the outset of World War II. The insights from that research, combined with my longstanding interest and (as a judge) activity in constitutional law, have moved me, and I hope equipped me, to write this book.

Not all national emergencies are consequences of war or terrorism. I mentioned the Great Depression. Natural disasters, too, can create emergency conditions that invite legally and even constitutionally problematic responses. Imagine strict quarantining and compulsory vaccination in response to a pandemic, or the imposition of martial law in response to a catastrophic earthquake, volcanic eruption, tsunami, or asteroid strike. When New Orleans was inundated as a result of Hurricane Katrina in the late summer of 2005, proposals to use soldiers to help maintain law and order met objections based on long-standing fears of military intervention in domestic crises, fears that had been codified in an 1878 law called the Posse Comitatus Act. The act had signaled the end of the post–Civil War Reconstruction era by making it a crime to use the federal armed forces (as distinct from the state militias—the National Guard) for law enforcement unless an act of Congress expressly authorizes such use. Invocation of the Posse Comitatus Act was actually just an excuse for inaction in the New Orleans emergency because an act of Congress (the Stafford Act) *does* authorize the use of the armed forces to assist in emergencies. More fundamentally, in conditions of great danger legalistic limitations fall by the wayside; officials act, leaving the legal consequences to be sorted out later.

Indeed, if interpreted to prevent the president from responding effectively to a major emergency, the Posse Comitatus Act might be deemed an unconstitutional limitation on sovereign power and executive prerogative. In *United States v. Curtiss-Wright Export Corp.* (1936), the Supreme Court held that the United States acquired the powers of a sovereign nation by its successful revolution against Great Britain rather than by a grant in the Constitution; the nation is prior to the Constitution. National defense, not limited to defense against human enemies, is a core sovereign power and moreover one that traditionally is exercised by the executive. The particular context of *Curtiss-Wright* was the nation's foreign relations. But the principle of the case—that national power is not limited to the powers explicitly granted by the Constitution—is broader, and anyway our main terrorist enemies are foreign nonstate groups that pose a threat to the nation greater than that of most foreign states.

The Katrina-begotten controversy over the Posse Comitatus Act illustrates how emergencies can squeeze civil liberties. The national security measures adopted after the 9/11 attacks provide many other illustrations of the squeeze; I have sought to anchor my analysis in them.

The core meaning of "civil liberties" is freedom from coercive or otherwise intrusive governmental actions designed to secure the nation against real or, sometimes, imagined internal and external enemies. The concern is that such actions may get out of hand, cre-

ating a climate of fear, oppressing the innocent, stifling independent thought, and endangering democracy. Civil liberties can even
be thought of as weapons of national security, since the government,
with its enormous force, is, just like a foreign state, a potential enemy of the people. Civil liberties are also means of bringing the judiciary into the national security conversation, with a perspective that
challenges that of the national security experts. The separation of
powers has epistemic as well as political significance: competition
among branches of government can stimulate thought, correct errors, force experts to explain themselves, expose malfeasance, and
combat slack and complacency.

But the more numerous or dangerous the nation's enemies are
believed to be, the greater the pressure to curtail civil liberties in
favor of executive discretion and unity of command, in order to enable the government to wield its great power more effectively, if less
responsibly. The traditional internal enemies are criminals, though
in the Civil War they were rebels. The traditional external enemies
are foreign states. But at present, with U.S. crime rates well below
their historic highs and no major power posing a significant military
threat to the nation, the external enemies whom Americans mainly
fear are Islamist terrorists. And with good reason: they are numerous, fanatical, implacable, elusive, resourceful, resilient, utterly ruth-
less, seemingly fearless, apocalyptic in their aims, and eager to get
their hands on weapons of mass destruction and use them against us.
They did us terrible harm on September 11, 2001, and may do us
worse harm in the future. We know little about their current number, leaders, locations, resources, supporters, motivations, and plans;
and in part because of our ignorance, we have no strategy for defeat-
ing them, only for fighting them. Although our invasion of Afghanistan shortly after the 9/11 attacks and our subsequent vigorous
counterterrorist efforts have scattered the leadership of al-Qaeda, as
well as depriving the movement of its geographic base (though it has

obtained a quasi-sanctuary in Pakistan), we are far from victory. Indeed, it is arguable that we have lost ground since 9/11—that the spectacular success of the 9/11 attacks did more to turn the Muslim world against the West than the vigorous military and police response to Islamist terrorism has done to weaken the terrorist movement. Yet all this is speculation. For all we know, we may be quite safe. But we cannot afford to act on that optimistic assumption.

I call the Islamist terrorists external enemies because very few of them, it appears, are American citizens or even residents of the United States (though the few who are may be especially dangerous). They are neither rebels nor common criminals. But they differ from our previous external enemies, such as the Axis powers in World War II and the Soviet Union during the Cold War, and even for that matter the Confederacy in the Civil War, because those enemies opposed us with organized military forces. They operated through subversion as well as military confrontation—quite serious subversion during the Civil War and the early years of the Cold War (and before—in fact, Soviet penetration of the U.S. government peaked during World War II). But the primary threats were military. A military enemy can usually be fought with minimal impairment of civil liberties beyond conscription and the censorship of militarily sensitive information. But terrorists do not field military forces that we can grapple with in the open. And they are not content to operate against us abroad; they penetrate our country by stealth to kill us. Rooting out an invisible enemy in our midst might be fatally inhibited if we felt constrained to strict observance of civil liberties designed in and for eras in which the only serious internal threat (apart from spies) came from common criminals.

But just as attacks by terrorists or foreign nations are not the only source of national emergencies, so not all forms of terrorism create national emergencies warranting the curtailment of existing rights. The tendency to equate any politically motivated violent crime with terrorism should be resisted. Many such crimes, such as those committed by animal-rights fanatics, are no more dangerous than run-of-the-mill crimes. My concern is limited to terrorism that has the potential to create a national emergency. This qualification should be borne in mind throughout the book.

Subversive activities during the Civil War and the Cold War begot severe responsive measures, such as suspension of habeas corpus in the earlier struggle and the prosecution of communist leaders in the later one. In the wake of 9/11 the federal government adopted measures that at first encountered little resistance from the public or politicians but since have become controversial as the attacks recede in time and the anxiety caused by them concomitantly diminishes. The measures and the initial acquiescence in them by the public were the predictable responses to a sudden sharp increase in a perceived threat to the nation's safety. The central question addressed in this book is how far civil liberties based on the Constitution should be permitted to vary with the threat level.

The qualification "based on the Constitution" requires emphasis. Many protections of civil liberties are of purely statutory origin. The Posse Comitatus Act is one example. The right of convicted criminals to obtain judicial review by means of habeas corpus is another; the Constitution limits suspension of habeas corpus, but the right of habeas corpus thus presupposed is, as we'll see in Chapter 3, more limited than the statutory right. A third example is the statutory right of a college student to insist that his grades not be disclosed to a prospective employer. Some civil liberties protections originate in treaties, such as the Convention Against Torture, to which the United States is a party. It is a mistake to think that "constitutional" is a compliment. Much that the government is permitted by the Constitution to do it should not do and can be forbidden to do by legislation or treaties. Constitutional law is intended to be a loose garment; if it binds too tightly, it will not be adaptable to changing circumstances and will leave too little room for the play of democratic forces. The analysis in this book is limited to constitutional law, so from now on, unless otherwise indicated, when I use the term "civil liberties" I mean "civil liberties derived from the Constitution."

A related point is the distinction between right and power. One way to oppose an exertion of legislative or executive power is to argue that it violates rights. But another is to argue that it simply exceeds the lawful power of the legislature or the executive. A local business firm that Congress attempts to regulate can object that Article I of the Constitution, which authorizes Congress to regulate interstate and foreign commerce, doesn't authorize it to regulate a purely local business. But it would be a stretch to argue that the regulation invaded a constitutional *right*. Unauthorized action is not necessarily the infringement of a *right*. My subject is constitutional rights, so I shall not be concerned with limitations on government power that do not protect such rights. But I will be very concerned with constitutionally conferred powers of government that limit those rights. The scope of governmental power to take actions to protect national security is the reciprocal of the individual's rights to liberty and privacy. So this is a book about the Constitution, not just about constitutional rights.

Although the title of this book evokes a history of emergency measures that goes back to the founding of the nation, this is not a work of history. Thus I am not much interested in what rights rebels and their sympathizers might have in a civil war. The threat of another civil war is not what is placing pressure on constitutional rights today. The pressure is coming mainly, though not entirely, from the threat of terrorism in a world increasingly menaced by weapons of mass destruction. (I shall generally term this the threat of "modern terrorism.") The question is how far this pressure should be resisted.

Chapter 1 discusses how constitutional rights are created and argues that the principal creators are not the actual draftsmen or ratifiers of the constitutional text but the justices of the Supreme Court, and that the justices are heavily influenced by the perceived practical consequences of their decisions rather than being straitjacketed by legal logic. As a result, constitutional law is fluid, protean, and responsive to the flux and pressure of contemporary events. The elasticity of constitutional law has decisive implications for the scope of constitutional rights during an emergency.

Chapter 2 applies the approach sketched in Chapter 1 to civil liberties, arguing that they are the point of balance between concerns for personal liberty and concerns for public safety. The former concerns are the basis of constitutional rights; the latter are the basis of government powers, which limit some rights (while, of course, creating many others, but statutory rights are not my subject) but which are as firmly grounded in constitutional values as constitutional rights are. It would be odd if the framers of the Constitution had cared more about every provision of the Bill of Rights than about national and personal survival. In times of danger, the weight of concerns for public safety increases relative to that of liberty concerns, and civil liberties are narrowed. In safer times, the balance shifts the other way and civil liberties are broadened. Civil libertarians disagree with this method of determining the scope of civil liberties; I explain in Chapter 2 why I think their approach flawed and their fears of a more flexible, practical approach unfounded.

Most civil libertarians look almost exclusively to the courts, and to constitutional law fashioned and enforced by courts, to safeguard civil liberties in periods of national emergency as at other times. Their court-centric approach is shortsighted. Judges, knowing little about the needs of national security, are unlikely to oppose their own judgment to that of the executive branch, which is responsible for the defense of the nation. They are especially unlikely to interpose *constitutional* objections because of the difficulty of amending the Constitution to correct judicial error. Conservative judges are particularly unlikely to resist claims of national security—and the federal judiciary may be more conservative today than at any other time in the last half century.

Fortunately, when national security measures are agreed on by Congress and the president, the need for judicial intervention diminishes. The legislative and executive branches are rivalrous even when nominally controlled by the same political party; the Republican Congress has not been a rubber stamp for the national security initiatives of the Bush administration. To an extent not acknowledged by civil libertarians, the Court can sit back and let the other branches duke it out, for when the competitive branches agree on a measure, the likelihood of its being an exaggerated response to a perceived danger is diminished.

The four succeeding chapters, Chapters 3 through 6, analyze the three principal sets of constitutional rights that come under pressure in times of real or imagined national emergency. I concentrate on the post-9/11 counterterrorist measures, actual and contemplated, that have engendered the most controversy. They include the attempt to deny the right of habeas corpus to captured terrorist suspects; the interception of phone calls and other electronic communications, such as e-mails, of U.S. citizens by the National Security Agency outside the limits set by the Foreign Intelligence Surveillance Act; ambitious data-mining projects such as the military's Able Danger project; demands by the FBI under section 215 of the USA PATRIOT Act for records of library borrowings; monitoring of the constitutionally protected speech of radical imams; torture or quasi-torture of terrorist suspects; and establishment of military tribunals to try suspected terrorists, including U.S. citizens apprehended in the United States rather than on a foreign field of combat such as Afghanistan or Iraq.

The general argument of these chapters is that the scope of constitutional liberties is rightly less extensive at a time of serious terrorist threats and rapid proliferation of means of widespread destruction than at a time of felt safety, but that the degree of curtailment required to protect us is not so great as to impair the feeling of freedom that is so important to Americans. It would leave intact the essential structure of constitutional liberties that the Supreme Court has been building since the 1950s and 1960s. That essential structure is one we can inhabit comfortably until the terrorist menace abates, however long that may be.

Chapters 3 and 4 discuss constitutional rights against the use of physical (and to a lesser extent psychological) coercion, whether to arrest or intern a person, deport or relocate him, search him or his home or seize his possessions, or obtain information from him by brutal measures up to and including torture. Chapter 3 examines the constitutional rights of people detained on suspicion of being terrorists to challenge their detention, particularly the right of habeas corpus and the right to due process of law. Chapter 4 examines constitutional rights that bear on the interrogation of detainees and on searches of terrorist suspects preceding detention. That chapter also discusses surreptitious electronic searches that, though they do not involve physical force or trespass, are generally though perhaps mistakenly considered to be subject to the same limitations that the Fourth Amendment to the Constitution places on conventional searches and seizures.

Much of the debate over how much force the government can employ against terrorists, how much snooping it can do, and so forth, without violating the Constitution, has revolved around the question of whether the United States is at war with terrorists or whether they are simply a particularly noxious form of political criminal. I argue that the terrorist threat is sui generis—that it fits the legal category neither of "war" nor of "crime." It requires a tailored regime, one that gives terrorist suspects fewer constitutional rights than people suspected of ordinary crimes, though not no rights. In particular, such suspects should have a constitutional right to demand, by applying to a court for habeas corpus, that a judicial officer determine whether their detention has a legal basis—the right, in other words, to due process of law.

Even torture may sometimes be justified in the struggle against terrorism, but it should not be considered *legally* justified. A recurrent theme of the book is that a nonlegal "law of necessity" that would furnish a moral and political but not legal justification for acting in contravention of the Constitution may trump constitutional rights in extreme situations. The limits of legal codification as a method of social control are especially acute in the context of national security; that is the lesson of the controversy over the scope and application of the Foreign Intelligence Surveillance Act to modern terrorism, as we shall see in Chapter 4.

Chapter 5 discusses three issues of free speech. The first is the propriety of investigating political extremists in this country, such as Muslim clergy who preach holy war against the United States, even if they do not actually recruit or incite terrorists. The second is whether to suppress rather than merely monitor such extremist speech. The third is how far newspapers, television, and other media should be forbidden to publicize sensitive information, including information concerning the rough tactics sometimes used by the government to fight terrorism, when the media learn about the tactics from government officials who disclosed classified information in violation of law.

I argue that it is constitutionally permissible to base noncoercive investigations on a group's political beliefs, provided that those beliefs are likely to endanger national security by encouraging terrorist activity. The effect of such investigations in deterring the free expression of political beliefs is undeniable but probably modest. Nor would such investigations or other forms of national security "profiling" constitute unconstitutional religious or ethnic discrimination.

It might even be constitutional to criminalize the expression of terrorism-promoting beliefs, rather than just conducting surveillance of their promoters, if such expression posed a serious, even though not imminent, threat to public safety. But that is an issue for the future; the case for punishing extremist Islamic expression in this country has not yet been made.

Regarding the third issue, that of censoring the media, I argue that an American version of the British Official Secrets Act may be needed in order to seal leaks of classified material that are harmful to national security or that invade personal privacy, and that such a law would not violate the Constitution. I also note that it may become necessary to censor the scholarly publication of biological research that might provide terrorists with detailed recipes for biological weapons.

Chapter 6 examines rights of privacy, with particular attention to the question whether a private individual should have a constitutional right to conceal from the government personal information that he has already disclosed voluntarily to strangers, such as banks, insurers, online bookstores, and other vendors of goods or services. I argue that the fact that an individual has surrendered some of his privacy to a vendor or other entity with which he deals need not be treated as a blanket waiver of all claims that he might want to make to the privacy of the information thus disclosed. The courts have not yet recognized the distinction because they do not think of informational privacy as a constitutional right separate from the rights conferred by constitutional provisions, such as the Fourth Amendment, that forbid particular methods of invading privacy. I argue further in that chapter, picking up a theme first sounded in Chapter 4, that mining the vast amount of personal information stored in public and private computer databases is a critical weapon against modern terrorism and can be employed with minimal harm to the types of privacy that people value most.

Chapters 5 and 6 are related because people require a degree of privacy in order to be able to develop and express politically unpopular beliefs that may have significant social value, as distinct from the beliefs of advocates of holy war against the United States. Those beliefs—the contentions of relativists notwithstanding—have no value, at least to us.

The Conclusion explores further the distinction between power in the sense of authority and power in the sense of raw ability to implement a policy choice. The government could be authorized by a constitutional amendment to curtail particular civil liberties in times of national emergency. But alternatively it could continue to be (as at present it is) denied that legal authority yet acknowledged to possess the power, and even the moral duty, to violate legal, including constitutional, rights when necessary to avoid catastrophic harm to the nation. Civil disobedience can be a duty of government in extreme circumstances to its citizens, even if not a right.

This is a book about law, and so it is for lawyers; it is about national security, and so it is also for students of national security and members of the national security community who are not lawyers. But it is also a book for the general reader. The issues it covers are important to all Americans, and there is nothing to prevent the issues from being made accessible to intelligent nonspecialists except the specialist's habit of communicating with other specialists in a private vocabulary. I have tried to fight the habit in this book, and in earnest of my intentions have eschewed footnotes and endnotes. The "Further Readings" suggested at the end of the book direct the reader to cases, statutes, books, and articles that either are mentioned in the book or provide helpful amplification or critique.

I thank Lindsey Briggs, Sarah Fackrell, Meghan Maloney, and Amy Moffett for their skillful research assistance and Larry Bernstein, Michael Boudin, Charles Fried, Scott Hemphill, Stephen Holmes, Jonathan Masur, Charlene Posner, Eric Posner, Frederick Schauer,

Geoffrey Stone, and Adrian Vermeule for invaluable comments on a previous draft. I also thank Jon Elster, Jeremy Waldron, and the other participants in a workshop on security/terrorism issues at Columbia University for their very helpful comments, as well as participants in the Constitutional Law Workshop of the University of Chicago Law School. The encouragement of this project by Geoffrey Stone and by Dedi Felman, my editor at Oxford University Press, deserves a special acknowledgment.

CHAPTER ONE

How Are Constitutional Rights Created?

IT IS NATURAL TO THINK that constitutional rights are rights stated in the text of the Constitution of the United States. But it is wrong, not completely but in an important sense. Constitutional rights are created mainly by the Supreme Court of the United States by "interpretation" of the constitutional text. I put the word in scare quotes because the line between judicial interpretation and judicial creation is frequently—particularly in the case of American constitutional law—fine to the point of invisibility.

The provisions that bear most directly on the issues discussed in this book are all found in either the original Constitution of 1787 or the Bill of Rights of 1789. For the most part either the provisions are vague, such as the Fourth Amendment's prohibition of "unreasonable" searches and seizures and the Fifth Amendment's prohibition against depriving a person of life, liberty, or property without "due process of law" (and what are the outer bounds of "liberty" and "property"?), or they have an eighteenth-century meaning that if strictly adhered to today would render them largely obsolete. For example, "searches" and "seizures" could not in 1789 have encompassed wiretapping or other electronic surveillance. Nor was there any notion then that the constitutional limitation on searches and seizures was based on a concern with privacy—or indeed any notion that privacy was an interest of constitutional dignity except in special circumstances such as the quartering of troops in private homes, a practice sharply limited by the Third Amendment. "Freedom of speech" probably just meant freedom from censorship (that was Blackstone's view), as distinct from immunity from punishment after the fact for speech determined by a jury to be blasphemous, seditious, defamatory, or otherwise intolerable. The right conferred by the Fifth Amendment not to be compelled to incriminate oneself had reference only to being compelled to give testimony under oath; it had nothing to do with coercing confessions or other statements outside the legal process even if they were used as evidence in a trial, or as leads to evidence. Obviously, global terrorism conducted with the aid of cell phones and the Internet and potentially utilizing weapons of mass destruction was not foreseen or expressly provided for anywhere in the Constitution.

The framers did include provisions regarding the conduct of war and the suppression of rebellion, as well as crime, with emphasis on criminal defendants' rights. But these provisions do not make a good match with the distinctive characteristics of modern terrorism, which defies conventional constitutional categories such as war and crime. Not only are rights that would block measures that the government might want to adopt to combat modern terrorism not clearly articulated in the Constitution, but governmental authority to employ such measures is not specified either. The framers were smart, but they were not demigods.

Because the Constitution is extremely difficult to amend, the pressure on the Supreme Court to interpret it loosely so as to keep it up to date is acute, in fact irresistible. The yielding to this felt pressure for *aggiornamento* is made easier by the fact that precisely because the Constitution is so difficult to amend, the Court need have little fear that its constitutional interpretations that modify earlier understandings will be nullified by adoption of new amendments to the Constitution to restore those understandings. In addition, the justices serve life terms and can be removed only by the cumbersome process of impeachment by the House of Representatives and conviction by the Senate. The finality of their decisions and the monarchical security of their tenure give the justices largely a free hand. And they need it. So much of the constitutional text is vague or obsolete that a great deal of judicial patchwork is required for the Constitution to remain serviceable more than two centuries after it was written. The need is especially acute in times of national emergency because it is virtually impossible to amend the Constitution quickly, and indeed unwise to try because the risk of error would be great.

Moreover, the justices are Americans, which means that they are not shrinking violets; they are not habituated to deference to authority, including the authority of an old piece of parchment written with ink drawn from a feather quill. It also means that they tend to be pragmatic (pragmatism is the American national culture), hence forward-looking rather than slaves to history. Anyway, they are lawyers rather than historians, and, being lawyers, treat history not as a guide but as a trove of anecdotes and rhetorical flourishes. And because they are trained in the common law, which is a body of law made by judges, it comes naturally to them to make constitutional law rather than just apply preexisting rules.

The breadth of the discretionary authority of Supreme Court justices is responsible for the intense public scrutiny that nominees to the Court undergo in their Senate confirmation hearings. Were justices technicians rather than policy makers, those hearings would be a lot shorter.

I don't mean to suggest, however, that the Court engages in as freewheeling an amendatory activity as the official amenders of the Constitution do—Congress and the states (or a constitutional convention). The justices' lack of democratic accountability makes them vulnerable to charges of judicial usurpation. To deflect these charges, the justices try to trace their innovations back to explicit directives in the constitutional text by a process called "reasoning by analogy." Wiretapping is not the same thing as rifling a person's desk, but it is analogous; prosecution for publishing a book that advocates revolution is analogous to a censor's refusing to license its publication in the first place. Proceeding by analogy maintains the appearance of connectedness to the constitutional text, enabling each new case to be given a pedigree and thus to be thought interpretive rather than creative. But both the literal and intended meaning of the original text may have been abandoned in the process. For reasoning by analogy is slippery. Invariably there is a choice of analogies. Advocacy of revolution could have been analogized to solicitation or incitement to crime rather than to political agitation. Wiretapping could have been analogized to eavesdropping, which has never been thought a Fourth Amendment violation (unless the eavesdropper was trespassing). The analogy could have been defended by noting that while a physical search disturbs the peace and quiet of the home, often leaving a mess, and frightens and humiliates the occupants, wiretapping does none of these things. And indeed initially, in the *Olmstead* case, decided in 1928, the Supreme Court held that wiretapping was not a search or a seizure.

For that matter, it is up to the justices to decide, whether in general or in particular cases, whether to proceed by analogy or by some other technique of legal reasoning—or not to proceed at all. It is easy to imagine judicial interpretations of the key provisions of the Constitution that would be much narrower—they once were much narrower—than those the modern Court has adopted, yet which would be just as plausible in terms of the orthodox materials of legal interpretation, such as original text and understandings, and often more so. (*Olmstead* is just one of hundreds of examples.) That is why the body of currently recognized constitutional rights is realistically regarded as more the handiwork of Supreme Court justices than of the Constitution's framers. And if justices are thus engaged in making rules that are only loosely tethered to constitutional text and history, the rules are bound to be heavily influenced by contemporary needs and conditions, just as formal legislation is. What judges make, judges can unmake. If constitutional law is shaped and honed by their responses to their contemporary circumstances, the law will change as circumstances change.

Judge-made law tends, however, to lag in its response to changed circumstances. This is a characteristic of legislation as well; the statute books are littered with obsolete statutes that owe their survival to the inertia of the legislative process. But a legislature can and sometimes does change course abruptly, with no felt sense of obligation to maintain continuity with previous legislation. Judges are more reluctant to overrule their "legislative" product, that is, their previous decisions. To do so is to acknowledge error (or at least the failure of foresight that has caused a previous decision to become obsolete), to undermine the stability of the law, to invite challenges to other decisions, and, particularly in constitutional cases, to drop the mask and reveal a court engaged in making legislative judgments. The impetus for overruling is likely to come from judges who had not yet been appointed when the overruled decision was rendered but, had they been, would have decided the case differently—not because they are better judges but because they have an ideology different from that of their predecessors. Adherence to precedent creates the impression that case law is the product of a consensus of generations of judges. Sometimes it is, but often it is the product of prudential factors that lead judges to adhere to predecessors' decisions for which they would never have voted.

Adherence to precedent is bound to be weaker in constitutional law than in statutory or common law because of the difficulty of amending a constitution, especially the U.S. Constitution. (An especially formidable obstacle is that three-fourths of the states must ratify an amendment for it to become effective.) The justices have no choice but to clean up after themselves. As a result, other than in the short run, adherence to precedent plays a distinctly limited role in U.S. constitutional law. The controversial parts of the Constitution are for the most part unchanged since the Fourteenth Amendment was ratified in 1868. The parts that generate controversy over national security measures taken by the federal government are unchanged since 1789, the date of the Bill of Rights. Yet constitutional law is starkly different today from what it was in 1789, or 1868, or indeed from what it was in 1935, 1950, or even 1960. What is sought to be conserved, by those who fear judges such as Justice Clarence Thomas, who is disdainful of precedent, is a body of revolutionary decisions made by the Supreme Court between the early 1960s and the middle 1970s, decisions correctly recognized by critics at the time as having no pedigree. They were exercises of political will rather than of professional judgment—which is not to deny that they continue to exert a considerable influence over the Court because of stare decisis.

I need to be more precise about the sense in which constitutional law may be said to be "starkly different" today from what it was in times past, especially the recent past. The perceived rapidity and magnitude of legal change depend on the level of generality at which the description of a body of law is pitched. At the highest level, there is no change. The Fourth Amendment forbade unreasonable searches and seizures in 1791 (the date of ratification); it forbids unreasonable searches and seizures today. At a slightly lower level of generality, the Fourth Amendment *has* changed: evidence obtained in violation of it cannot be used at trial; a warrant is presumptively required, though there are many exceptions to the requirement; wiretapping and other forms of electronic eavesdropping are deemed searches and seizures—all these are rules that long postdate 1791. Even at the lower level of generality, it is possible to argue that national emergencies alter not the right but merely its application. But it is more accurate to say that a national emergency may alter the *scope* of a right, and from a practical standpoint it is the scope rather than the mere existence of a right that is important.

The vaguer or more general the constitutional text and precedents that create and define the right, the more elastic its scope, enabling judges to change that scope without overruling any precedent and thus in a sense (though an artificial one) without changing the law. But even when a precedent is quite precise—a pertinent example is the *Brandenburg* decision (1969), discussed in Chapter 5, which appears to place tight limits on when advocacy can be punished—the Court can usually get around it by emphasizing contextual factors that have emerged since the decision. The upshot is that the justices usually can change the law without the visible perturbation that accompanies an explicit overruling.

So how best to describe a judicial decision made by judges—the Supreme Court justices—who are not subject to being overruled by a higher court, are not tightly bound by precedent, and are not interpreting a clear, up-to-date, and therefore definitive text that could be laid alongside their decisions to provide a benchmark for determining whether the decision was correct or incorrect? Because of the antiquity and nebulousness of key constitutional provisions, and also because of their own immunity from being reversed (as Justice Robert Jackson once remarked, Supreme Court justices are not final because they are infallible, but infallible because they are final), the justices are free from even the loose constraints under which other federal judges labor, and so by default find themselves making decisions in much the same way that other Americans do—by balancing the anticipated consequences of alternative outcomes and picking the one that creates the greatest preponderance of good over bad effects. Though the justices are cabined to some extent by the traditions of the bench and a perceived lack of democratic legitimacy, their discretion is very broad and within its capacious limits the judgments the justices make, not being determined by authoritative legal materials or generated by some tightly logical or scientific mode of reasoning—"legal reasoning" in a sense analogous to the methods of exact inquiry employed in logic, mathematics, and the natural sciences—are best described as policy judgments. In novel cases, cases that have no direct precedent, the significance of previously decided cases is merely as a repository of facts and insights that may help the judges in the new case make a sensible policy judgment.

So a Supreme Court justice asked to decide whether someone detained by the U.S. military outside U.S. territorial limits can seek habeas corpus from an American court is likely to proceed by comparing the effects of answering yes with the effects of answering no. The yes will increase the protection of personal liberty by reducing the likelihood of a mistaken detention but will reduce public safety by making it more difficult for the military to detain people whom it considers a threat to the nation. Not that the threat is certain to materialize if the court answers yes, but public safety is diminished when the risks to it increase; probabilistic menaces must be weighed along with certain ones.

Unfortunately, the "weighing" is usually metaphorical. The consequences judges consider are imponderables, and the weights assigned to them are therefore inescapably subjective. Each judge brings to the balancing process preconceptions that may incline him to give more weight to inroads on personal liberty than to threats to public safety, while another judge, bringing different preconceptions to the case, would reverse the weights. The weights are influenced by personal factors, such as temperament (whether authoritarian or permissive), moral and religious values, life experiences that may have shaped those values and been shaped by temperament, and sensitivities and revulsions of which the judge may be quite unaware.

Senate confirmation hearings for Supreme Court nominees are protracted and heated not so much because American constitutional law is policy called by the name of law but because it is not a policy science. There is little to stabilize it when the composition of the Court is diverse. The law will fluctuate with changes in personnel unless the successor justices happen to think the same way as their predecessors, which has been rare. When judicial decisions in areas of judge-made law, such as the common law, can be said to be "objective," it is not because legal reasoning enforces a uniform answer to the legal issues presented to the judges; it is because the judges happen to think alike.

The theory of Supreme Court decision making that I am expounding will be challenged at one end of the theory spectrum by those, mainly political scientists, who believe that Supreme Court justices can be divided into "liberals" and "conservatives" and their decisions predicted from their classification, as in the case of ordinary legislators, and at the opposite end by those—call them formalists—who believe that decisions by the Supreme Court are the product of a rigorous, impersonal, essentially deductive process applied in good faith, if not always with complete success, to the Constitution's text. The process is conceived as one in which there is no role for the political preferences (broadly or narrowly construed) of the individual justices and no regard for the consequences of their decisions. Thus, *fiat iustitia ruat caelum*—let justice be done even if the heavens fall.

In between is the view of most constitutional theorists, who believe that the justices cast their votes on the basis of reasonable metaprinciples consistently applied. They might be moral or religious principles (versions of natural law), the intentions of the framers, some broader sense of the eighteenth-century political culture from which the text emerged, principles derived from precedents, a ruling political principle deemed latent in the constitutional text (typical candidates being Justice Stephen Breyer's concept of "active liberty" and the late John Hart Ely's concept of "representation-reinforcing" judicial review), or a concept of the proper balance among the different branches of government derived from notions of relative judicial, executive, and legislative competence or legitimacy. But there is no consensus on which metaprinciple should prevail in the event of a conflict or indeed on which if any of them are valid.

The sheer multitude of alternative approaches to constitutional decision making and the interminability of the debates among their advocates are evidence that constitutional theory is deeply subjective, providing therefore no solid guidance to Supreme Court justices and so leaving them to make up constitutional law as they go along, in the usual way in which practical people make decisions: on the basis of anticipated consequences refracted through life experience and other personal factors.

To suggest that the justices bring preconceptions to the task of adjudication may seem to accuse them of bias. Not so. All orderly thinking proceeds from preconceptions (Bayesian "priors"). A tabula rasa theory of judging—though proclaimed by many judges, as when they say in deciding a statutory case that they begin with the words of the statute—is a cognitive impossibility. Judges start with a sense of what the case is about and what the statute is about before starting to parse the statute. Judicial bias in the pejorative sense means taking account of considerations, such as a litigant's race or politics, that clearly should not be allowed to shape a judge's preconceptions.

Though lacking firm moorings in constitutional text, precedent, or metaprinciple, American judges are not predestined to be judicial activists. If "judicial activism" is not to be merely a general term of disapprobation, it should be limited to a court's seeking to aggrandize itself at the expense of other branches of government—as the Supreme Court did during the chief justiceship of Earl Warren; as it had earlier done in the *Lochner* era, when the Court ran wild with the judge-made concept of liberty of contract; and as it was later to do with the judge-made concept of sexual and reproductive privacy. The greatest judges in U.S. history, such as Oliver Wendell Holmes, Benjamin Cardozo, Learned Hand, and Robert Jackson, were none of them activists in this sense. And for a good pragmatic reason. When the Supreme Court in the name of the Constitution invalidates the act of another branch of government, it stifles a social experiment. By doing so it deprives itself as well as the nation of critical information concerning the consequences of the experiment for liberty, privacy, safety, diversity, or other values. It's as if a scientist said: "Your hypothesis may be correct, but I don't like it, so I'm not going to test it." If judges are to learn the consequences of social policy, they must walk the executive and legislative branches of government on a long leash. Of course, some experiments are not worth trying, some are blocked by uncontroversial understandings of the limits that the Constitution places on government, and some have been allowed to run long enough to enable their merits to be evaluated without a further period of testing. (It is a virtue of our constitutional system that the courts can't rule on a policy unless and until a case is brought by someone harmed by the policy.) But when in doubt about the actual or likely consequences of a measure, the pragmatic, empiricist judge will be inclined to give the other branches of government their head. Such a judge is therefore more likely to be a practitioner of judicial self-restraint than a judicial activist. It is the dogmatists of the Right or the Left, indifferent to consequences and insensitive to the weaknesses of legal reasoning, who are most likely to be judicial activists.

Even if I am right that the justices, or at least most of them, most of the time, in the key cases, base their decisions on a balancing of anticipated consequences, pro and con, it doesn't follow that the system of constitutional rights that they have created is the best that can be imagined. They may have placed the wrong weights on particular consequences, perhaps reflecting a professional deformation— lawyers are habituated to talking about rights and liberty, not power and national security. Or, swerving the other way, they may have been unduly credulous about the government's claims regarding the imperatives of national security. Or they may have been too much in thrall to precedents that either were unsound when created or have become obsolete as a result of changed political, social, economic, or technological circumstances.

This last concern—thralldom to precedent—might play a major role in an assessment of a mature body of constitutional law but has limited significance in the context of today's national security crisis. The threat of global terrorism, as sketched all too briefly in the Introduction, is novel. The case law addressing constitutional rights affected by measures to meet the terrorist threat is in its infancy. It is true that, so wedded are American lawyers to case law, when they are faced with a novel issue they will reach back as far as necessary to find a case to cite as "authority" for resolving the issue. They may cite *Ex parte Milligan* for the proposition that military tribunals cannot be used to try U.S. civilians (more broadly, that martial law cannot be imposed) as long as the regular courts are open. *Ex parte Milligan* was decided in 1866. The idea that a case almost a century and half old should guide us in dealing with al-Qaeda is ridiculous, as I think most of the Supreme Court justices would acknowledge, at least sotto voce. Not that hauling civilian U.S. citizens before military tribunals isn't something to worry about. But we don't need an ancient case to tell us that. Would civil libertarians fold their tents if the Supreme Court had allowed Milligan to be executed? Recent cases, some of which I will be citing, provide better, though far from infallible, guidance to solving modern problems.

The task is thus not to criticize an existing body of law focused on the matter at hand—it is a skinny body—but to suggest the direction that the law should take, by assessing the relevant consequences and hoping that the Supreme Court will be convinced by the assessment and shape the law accordingly. That is the main task of this book.

CHAPTER TWO

How Does National Security Shape Constitutional Rights?

THE CHALLENGE to constitutional decision making in the era of modern terrorism is to restrike the balance between the interest in liberty from government restraint or interference and the interest in public safety, in recognition of the grave threat that terrorism poses to the nation's security. The scope of a right must be calibrated by reference to the interests that support and oppose it. But how to do this? Ideally, in the case of a right (for example, the right to be free from unreasonable searches and seizures) that could be asserted against government measures for protecting national security, one would like to locate the point at which a slight expansion in the scope of the right would subtract more from public safety than it would add to personal liberty and a slight contraction would subtract more from personal liberty than it would add to public safety. That is the point of balance, and determines the optimal scope of the right. The point shifts continuously as threats to liberty and safety wax and wane. At no time can the exact point be located. Yet to imagine it the object of our quest is useful in underscoring that the balance between liberty and safety must be struck at the margin. One is not to ask whether liberty is more or less important than safety. One is to ask whether a particular security measure harms liberty more or less than it promotes safety.

Judgment will be influenced by an overall assessment of the importance of liberty vis-à-vis safety, however, because marginal weights are influenced by total weights. And that overall assessment will differ among Supreme Court justices. Some will attach transcendent value to personal liberty, others to safety. Those in the former camp often make light of risks to safety in order to lighten the burden of decision. Similarly, those in the latter, the "safety first" camp, often slight the importance of civil liberties, again to avoid having to make agonizing choices. People inclined one way or another on some issue tend to exaggerate the cogency of the arguments that support their inclination because they want to feel confident that they are making the right choice, that it is not a toss-up. No one likes to be in a state of doubt, and people have psychological defenses against being forced into such a state. But there are real disagreements as well. Some students of constitutional law, for example, think that conferring constitutional rights on criminals and terrorists has value in itself; others, that it has value only as an instrument for protecting the innocent. Some think the terrorist threat is very great, others that it is greatly exaggerated, and this disagreement will affect judgment as to the appropriate scope of constitutional protection of terrorist suspects even if there is no disagreement over the value or importance of civil liberties in general.

The optimal balance between liberty and security depends not only on the weights assigned to the competing values but also on the effect on those values of the safety measure in question. A large reduction in security can dominate a small reduction in liberty even if liberty is thought much more valuable than security. Suppose liberty is worth 1,000 and security only 100; nevertheless, a 20 percent reduction in security as a result of invalidating some defensive measure (such as detaining terrorist suspects incommunicado) will cause more harm ($100 \times .20 = 20$) than a 1 percent reduction in liberty as a result of upholding the measure ($1,000 \times .01 = 10$). But to avoid the psychological discomfort of having to choose between alternatives that seem equally good, a judge who attaches a high value to liberty is likely to think the harm to liberty of a challenged security measure great and the boost to safety small, though a particular measure might have little impact on liberty yet enhance public safety significantly; and of course it is possible to overvalue particular liberties.

In conventional legal terms, the marginal approach equates to decision making guided by a standard and its rejection to decision making guided by a rule. Negligence is a standard, applied in particular cases by balancing the expected accident cost (the cost if the accident occurs discounted by the probability that it will occur) against the cost of preventing the accident; if the former is greater than the latter, the injurer is negligent and therefore liable. A fixed numerical speed limit is a rule, although a rule with exceptions, such as for police cars and other emergency vehicles. Rules, especially ones that allow of no exceptions, are simpler to apply than standards. But by making the outcome of a case depend on one or a few facts (such as the speed at which a car is traveling) rather than on all the relevant circumstances (which might include the design of the highway, the amount of traffic, the time of day, weather conditions, the driver's skills, and the reason he was speeding), rules often make a poor fit with the particular circumstances in which they are applied, and when this is so, exceptions may be allowed in order to improve the fit.

Civil libertarians generally want the constitutionality of security measures to be determined by rules rather than standards, for example the rule that political speech can be suppressed only if it contains an incitement to crime. They worry that standards will give the judges too much latitude to defer to restrictive measures imposed by Congress or the president. But they want the *rule* to be based on liberty and only the *exception* on safety. A public safety exception to a civil libertarian rule provides less protection for national security, as we shall see when we come to the rule of the *Brandenburg* case in Chapter 5, than a standard in which neither liberty nor safety has priority.

Although governance by a standard is often unworkable because too many factors are relevant or because the factors are too subjective to be weighed and compared, cases involving a clash between liberty and safety cannot yet be governed by rules. Rules would inevitably favor one over the other, and not enough is known at present to make a categorical judgment on which way to tilt a rule. Better for now, at least, to govern by standard, with the judges feeling their way over the new constitutional terrain created by the 9/11 attacks and the government's responses, deciding cases narrowly, preferably on statutory grounds, hesitating to trundle out the heavy artillery of constitutional invalidation. Eventually, as not only the nature of the terrorist threat but also the consequences for civil liberties of the post-9/11 security measures become clearer, it may become possible to crystallize sensible rules from the standard.

Accurate balancing of competing values requires courts to pay serious attention to risks rather than always insisting on certainty. It would be a mistake to think that a particular measure should be rejected because we do not know whether another terrorist attack on the United States will occur unless that measure is taken and so we cannot be certain that it will actually increase safety. Most safety measures are aimed at reducing risks rather than eliminating certainties, but that doesn't make the measures unwarranted. The fact that one cannot know whether interrogating a particular terrorist will ward off an attack does not make interrogating terrorists valueless. This point is obscured when there is a certain harm on one side of the balance and an uncertain benefit on the other. A terrorist subjected to torture incurs a harm with certainty. But that the torture will yield a benefit for national security is only a probability when the torture begins. The torture may be ineffective either because the person tortured has no useful information to impart or because he is able to withstand the torture; in either case, moreover, he may send his interrogators off on a wild-goose chase by lying.

While probabilistic benefits must not be ignored, they must be discounted by the probability that they will actually materialize. The expected value of a 10 percent chance of winning a $100 bet is only $10. But $10 is not zero. Civil libertarians emphasize probabilistic effects as much as national security experts do. They are concerned less with the impact of a curtailment of civil liberties on the particular individuals whose liberties are curtailed (say, a person investigated because of his political beliefs) than with the impact on features of the social landscape as a whole, such as the long-run vigor of political discourse. If the risk that terrorism poses to national security is speculative, so is the risk that counterterrorist measures pose to liberty.

Issues of institutional competence intrude at this point. Judges may lack confidence—and may be right to lack confidence—that they know enough about the consequences of particular measures taken for the protection of national security to be able to strike a proper balance. Judges think they know a lot about trading off liberty against safety in ordinary criminal cases. But they would admit they're not experts on national security in general or the terrorist threat in particular. The reasons they are not, and cannot become, experts on these subjects are twofold. First, the judiciary, unlike the executive and legislative branches, has no machinery for systematic study of a problem. Its staffs are small. It has to wait until it has a case to begin its inquiry into the facts and policy ramifications, and the pressure of its caseload requires it to decide the case without being able to take the time to study background and circumstances and likely consequences. If the case involves a subject such as contracts or accidents or ordinary crimes in which the court has long experience, its epistemic limitations will not be serious. But if, as in cases involving modern terrorism, the subject is new, the court will not have the time or resources to bone up on it. And second, our judges, including Supreme Court Justices, are generalists. Cases involving national security are only a tiny part of their docket. They cannot afford to devote much time to them.

The resulting knowledge deficit may incline judges confronting national security cases, depending on the judges' ideology, temperament, and intuition about relative risks, either to defer to the executive branch, where the relevant expertise largely resides, or to take an adversary stance. Yet even those judges who are suspicious of the security organs may hesitate to act on their suspicions in the face of strong public fears for safety. And even those inclined to defer to the executive branch may hesitate to do so, realizing that the executive branch wants to augment its power and is sometimes actuated by base political concerns, sheer impatience, or an excessively executive-centric perspective rather than by a balanced conception of the public interest. National security work tends, moreover, to select for people who place less weight on civil liberties than judges do.

In this clash of perspectives, it is unclear why a judicial perspective should rule, especially since judicially defined rights are only one check on executive overreaching. The separation of the executive and legislative powers is another. Unlike a parliamentary system, in which executive and legislative powers are fused, American government places those powers in competition with each other. Even when the executive and legislative branches are controlled by the same party, there is no unified control, because party discipline is weak. As Samuel Issacharoff and Richard Pildes argue, echoing Justice Robert Jackson's concurring opinion in *Youngstown Sheet & Tube Co. v. Sawyer* (1952), judges inclined to defer to the executive in matters of national security can take comfort from the fact, when it is a fact, that Congress has concurred in authorizing the challenged security measure—that it was not just an executive initiative. Recalling the hornet's nest stirred up in Congress by revelations of the Bush administration's warrantless interceptions of foreign communications of U.S. citizens in apparent violation of the Foreign Intelligence Surveillance Act, the successful resistance of influential members of Congress to renewing the USA PATRIOT Act without modification, and the flap over the mistreatment of detainees seized in the struggle against terrorism, one realizes that Congress is not a patsy even when, as in these instances, it is controlled by members of the same political party as the presidency and even when it is the Republican Party, the more disciplined of the two major parties.

A further argument for a light judicial hand in national security matters, at least when the president and the Congress concur on a national security measure, is that while few members of Congress are genuine experts on national security, the total amount of national security expertise in Congress (including congressional staff) is vastly greater than that in the judiciary. Judges aren't *supposed* to know much about national security; at least they don't think they are supposed to know much about it. A related reason for judges to defer to the judgment of the other branches of government in cases of doubt is that the efficacy—the consequences generally—of a security measure adopted to deal with a novel threat cannot be determined if the measure is blocked early on by a constitutional interpretation. The post-9/11 responses to the newly apprehended terrorist threat are entitled to a chance to prove themselves—good or bad.

An important implication of the principle that safety and liberty must be balanced at the margin is that the consequences of particular measures for the protection of national security must be considered in relation to alternative measures that might be taken instead. To argue that the information that could be extracted by torturing terrorists would increase public safety more than it would decrease the "liberty" (in a broad sense) of the tortured person assumes that the information could not be obtained by means that would do less harm to personal liberty. If it could, the incremental benefit of torture would be slight. But the incremental harm might also be rather slight, since forms of coercive interrogation that would not be considered to rise to the level of torture might nevertheless inflict significant emotional distress on the people subjected to them.

The case of torture brings to the fore an important general issue discussed further in the next chapter and in the Conclusion. It concerns the distinction between *authority* and *power*. In evaluating the argument for authorizing government to resort to torture in extreme circumstances (somehow defined)—as advocated, for example, by Alan Dershowitz in his book *Why Terrorism Works*—we must consider the alternative of simply recognizing that in desperate circumstances, as when a terrorist has information that is absolutely vital to averting a catastrophic attack, government *will* torture—will indeed be under a moral duty to torture—and that reliance on the executive's willingness to exercise raw power in extreme circumstances may be preferable to recognizing a legal right to do so. (The difference between private and public moral duties is one of the themes of my book *An Affair of State.*) That is, the *incremental* benefit to the public safety of recognizing a legal right, however circumscribed, to engage in torture, and a corresponding curtailment of the constitutional right not to be tortured, may be outweighed by the incremental harm that such recognition would do to liberty. The comparison is of increments because, even if no legal right to torture is recognized, the raw power to torture remains and will be exercised in extreme circumstances.

The fact that judges have to consider whether a legal right to torture should ever be recognized illustrates the important point that proper balancing of competing values in constitutional decision making is not shortsighted. Over and above the immediate consequences of a decision, we want judges to give weight to the social value of respecting the integrity of an authoritative legal instrument, such as the Constitution. It is one thing to say that "freedom of speech" is a vague term that can expand and contract accordion-like as circumstances dictate. It is another to say that the president can suspend the First Amendment during a national emergency. Perhaps he can do *anything* if the emergency is dire enough—the *Curtiss-Wright* principle mentioned in the Introduction. But there is no handle in the constitutional text for the unilateral assumption of dictatorial powers by the president, no matter how desperate the circumstances. We don't want the Constitution to be *just* an old piece of parchment.

Here is another example, and incidentally a bow to the lessons of history. The Constitution authorizes Congress to suspend habeas corpus "when in cases of Rebellion or Invasion the public Safety may require it," but nowhere says that the president can suspend it. Suspending habeas corpus is a terrifying power; it enables the government to imprison people at will and prevents them from challenging their imprisonment in court. It is understandable that the framers of the Constitution should have wanted to require, in effect, congressional concurrence in any decision by the president to assume such an awesome power. Nevertheless, Abraham Lincoln suspended habeas corpus (though in individual cases rather than across the board) at the outset of the Civil War without consulting Congress. Congress was not in session, and there is an argument for recognizing an implicit presidential authority to suspend habeas corpus when Congress is unable to do so but the public safety requires that it be done. (The argument would be stronger if Congress was incapable of convening—for example, because of a nuclear or biological attack on Washington.) But suppose Congress was in session and refused to suspend habeas corpus and the president went ahead and did so himself. He might have a compelling reason, but judges would rightly hesitate to acknowledge an extratextual executive authority of such scope. Lincoln himself claimed inherent authority to violate one constitutional provision (the suspension provision) in order to save the Constitution as a whole, so that he wasn't *really* violating the Constitution. But as there is no such grant of authority in the Constitution, this was just a lawyer's way of saying that it's okay to violate the Constitution if the need is dire enough, which is not a legal argument.

The balancing approach that I am advocating to determining the scope of constitutional rights in emergency circumstances highlights the *dynamic* character of constitutional law—the fact that the scope of a constitutional right changes as the relative weights of liberty and safety change. The change may be slow because courts move slowly, in part because of the drag that precedent exerts on judicial innovation. But change there will be. The low crime rate in the 1950s set the stage for the Supreme Court in the 1960s to multiply the rights of criminal defendants; then crime rates rose rapidly (whether or not because of that multiplication) and there was a backlash and the Court curtailed defendants' rights both directly, by redefining constitutional rights, and indirectly, by upholding congressional limitations on those rights. The safer the nation feels, the greater the weight that the courts place on personal liberty relative to public safety. When the nation feels endangered, the balance shifts the other way. The nation felt much safer before the 9/11 attacks than after, just as it felt much safer after the Cold War ended than before, and after the Civil War ended than while it was raging.

Neither in the case of soaring crime rates nor in that of an increased threat of terrorism are judges willing to say that rights are sacrosanct and the nation must either accept greater danger or find some other way to respond. The other ways may be ineffectual or prohibitively costly, and in the crunch most people put safety ahead of liberty. Of course, what the normally self-interested person wants most to do is to put *his* safety ahead of *your* liberty. But when that is not an option, he will usually accept restrictions on his liberty more readily than he will accept enhanced danger to his physical security. Moreover, the people at risk from crime and terrorism are far more numerous than those who face a higher risk of being falsely accused when protections of civil liberties are curtailed, provided they are curtailed only modestly.

It may be objected that a decision process based on a balancing of risks and harms is unworkable if the risks and harms cannot be measured. It is true that in the present setting they cannot be quantified. But we make pragmatic utility-maximizing decisions all the time without being able to quantify the costs and benefits of the alternatives among which we are choosing. You marry without being able to determine whether you might have met someone more suitable had you forgone this match. Many marriages fail, of course, and many judgments regarding the scope of civil liberties in times of national emergency are unsound. But we cannot avoid making such judgments and there is no good alternative to making them pragmatically.

THE SHARPEST CHALLENGE to the approach that I am sketching will come from civil libertarians. In a broad sense, almost all Americans are civil libertarians, that is, believers in a large sphere of freedom from government intrusion. But I denote by the term the adherents to the especially capacious view of civil liberties that is often advanced in litigation and lobbying by the American Civil Liberties Union.

Civil libertarians so defined are reluctant to acknowledge that national emergencies in general, or the threat of modern terrorism in particular, justify *any* curtailment of the civil liberties that were accepted on the eve of the emergency. They deny that civil liberties should wax and wane with changes in the danger level. They believe that the Constitution is about protecting individual rights rather than

about promoting community interests, a belief that some civil libertarians ground in a quasi-religious veneration of civil liberties coupled
with a profound suspicion of the coercive side of government—police,
prosecutors, the military, the intelligence community. (The small
civil libertarian Right, epitomized by the Cato Institute, extends this
suspicion to *all* activities of government.) They base that suspicion
on a belief, urged most recently in Geoffrey Stone's book *Perilous
Times*, that past curtailments of civil liberties were gratuitous responses to hysterically exaggerated fears. They believe that government always errs on the side of exaggerating threats to national
security. And so they believe that the current threat—the terrorist
threat—is exaggerated, perhaps deliberately by the Bush administration to promote its political fortunes, and that the laws and institutions in place on September 11, 2001, required no changes in order
to be adequate to cope with the current threat. They applaud the
words of Justice Hugo Black's concurring opinion in *New York Times
Co. v. United States* (1971) (the Pentagon Papers case): "the guarding
of military and diplomatic secrets at the expense of informed repre-
sentative government provides no real security for our Republic."
Implicitly they deny that the counterterrorism measures taken since
9/11 may be among the reasons that we haven't been attacked since.

Some civil libertarians (though not Professor Stone) believe that
any curtailment of civil liberties in time of emergency will continue
when the emergency passes; they believe, in other words, that there
is a civil liberties ratchet that might cause a succession of national
emergencies to culminate in tyranny. Others think that only rights
can limit rights—the right to an abortion can limit the expressive
rights of people who picket abortion clinics, but the public safety
cannot limit a right because there is no legally enforceable right to
police or military protection. And it is true that you can't sue the CIA
or the army for having failed to wipe out al-Qaeda before 9/11. But
the reason there is no legally enforceable right to security against

internal and external enemies is not that public safety is a lesser constitutional value than the values that inform the Bill of Rights. There is parity. The Constitution is much more than the Bill of Rights. The extensive powers that it confers on the president and Congress preeminently include the power to protect the nation from its enemies (to "provide for the common defence," as the preamble to the Constitution puts it). The constitutional powers are not legally enforceable only because making them so would thrust the courts deep into issues of resource allocation, which judges are ill equipped to resolve. It is much easier for judges to tell government what not to do than what to do.

Civil libertarians recognize that the values, communal in nature, that the powers of government are designed to protect are no less important than the individualist values that inform the legally enforceable constitutional rights. They vigorously defend executive power when bent to liberal ends (see the notable study by Elena Kagan), just as conservatives do when the power is deployed in the service of internal and external security. The importance of communal values is common ground; the disagreement is over which are the worthiest.

A belief of many civil libertarians that both jostles uneasily with their suspicion of police and prosecutors and, more important, reflects a misunderstanding of modern terrorism is that since acts of terrorism are criminal we should leave it to the criminal law to deal with them. So David Cole and Jim Dempsey want "intelligence" confined to "the collection and analysis of information about a [known] criminal enterprise" with the aim of using that information as evidence in a public trial of the criminals. They do not acknowledge that a public trial, or any trial, may come too late. The rather casual attitude of the FBI and other police forces toward ordinary crime—accepting that a great deal of it will occur and being content to limit the crime rate by apprehending and prosecuting a fraction of criminals, thus incapacitating some and deterring some others—is misplaced when it comes to fighting terrorism. Because terrorist attacks are potentially so destructive and also because many terrorists are undeterrable, the emphasis of public policy shifts from punishment after an attack occurs to preventing it from occurring. The line between punishment and prevention blurs when preparatory activity is criminalized, as it is in the criminal-law concepts of attempt and conspiracy. But civil libertarians want to limit the prosecution of preparatory activity, lest it result in punishment of harmless acts, as in the old English crime of "compassing" (imagining) the death of the king. A limitation to completed acts of terrorism, however, would make the criminal law an even less adequate response to terrorism than it is.

Civil libertarians are not always careful about history, perhaps because most of the rights they defend have no solid historical anchor, or perhaps because the lawyer's attitude toward history is a manipulative one (a tendency as pronounced on the legal Right, with its "originalist" fantasies, as on the Left). History does not confirm the existence of a civil liberties ratchet, a "slippery slope" on which the first step toward curtailing civil liberties precipitates an uninterrupted and perhaps accelerating decline. Every time civil liberties have been curtailed in response to a national emergency, whether real or imagined, they have been fully restored when the emergency passed—and in fact before it passed, often long before. That is another ignored lesson. Curtailments of civil liberties in the Civil War, World War II, and the Cold War were concentrated in the early periods of these crises. Cold War–era abuses by the CIA and the FBI declined steadily from Senator Joseph McCarthy's death in 1957 until the Nixon presidency, when they experienced a resurgence because of the turmoil stirred up by the Vietnam War, but they were then quickly curbed.

This pattern is no accident. At the outset of an emergency, the government is uncertain about its gravity, and on the principle that it is better to be safe than sorry reacts on a worst-case assumption. As more is learned about the danger, responsive measures are scaled down from worst case to best estimate. Most of the terrorist suspects, mainly illegal immigrants, rounded up and detained in the urgent sweeps that followed 9/11 were released after it became apparent that the 9/11 hijackers were not members of a vast internal network of suicide terrorists and their supporters. National security programs adopted by the president and Congress in the wake of the 9/11 attacks were, four years later, under siege.

Civil libertarians are the ratcheters, insisting that every increase in civil liberties should be treated as a platform for further increases. Because of decisions by the Supreme Court in the 1960s (the heyday of the Warren Court) and reactions to the Watergate scandal, the protection of civil liberties has expanded significantly since the 1950s. Yet even in the era of McCarthyism the United States was very far from being a police state. And such rollback of civil liberties as has occurred in the wake of the 9/11 attacks has not carried us back to anything like the 1950s. Resistance to any rollback, however slight— insistence, indeed, as in the "Law Professors' Petition," reendorsed by civil libertarians David Cole and Jim Dempsey *after* 9/11, on expanding civil liberties *beyond* the limits reached by the Supreme Court in the 1960s—is a defining characteristic of ACLU-style civil libertarianism.

Civil libertarians tend to slight significant historical episodes in which the nation was endangered by subversive activities that challenged the reigning concepts of civil liberties. One such episode was the Civil War, during which, as we know, Lincoln found it necessary to suspend habeas corpus and take other repressive measures against Confederate subversion. Another was the 1940s, when the Soviet

Union penetrated many federal agencies, unions, and other institutions and stole atomic secrets that accelerated Soviet acquisition of a nuclear capability. That acquisition in turn emboldened Stalin to encourage North Korea to invade South Korea, precipitating a war that killed thirty-six thousand American soldiers and more than two and a half million Koreans and Chinese. Domestic terrorism by Puerto Rican separatists, neo-Nazis, the Jewish Defense League, left-wing radicals such as the Weathermen, and al-Qaeda culminated in the truck bombing of the World Trade Center in 1993; in the destruction of the Oklahoma City federal building, killing 168 men, women, and children, by Timothy McVeigh and Terry Nichols in 1995; and, of course, in the 9/11 attacks. Conceivably the 9/11 attacks would have been prevented had the FBI not feared being turned down if it applied for a warrant to search the computer of Zacarias Moussaoui, a candidate to be one of the 9/11 hijack pilots.

Civil libertarians neglect a genuine lesson of history: that the greatest danger to American civil liberties would be another terrorist attack on the United States, even if it was on a smaller scale than the 9/11 attacks—but it could be on the same or even a much larger scale. The USA PATRIOT Act, which civil libertarians abhor, was passed within weeks of those attacks; it never would have passed, or in all likelihood even have been proposed, had the attacks been thwarted. The other novel measures that the government has adopted to combat the terrorist menace, and that civil libertarians denounce, also would not have been adopted had it not been for 9/11. A minor present curtailment of civil liberties, to the extent that it reduces the probability of a terrorist attack, reduces the likelihood of a major future curtailment of those liberties. I emphasize "minor" and "major." Obviously civil libertarians shouldn't applaud repressive measures that contribute to national security only trivially.

Civil liberties depend on national security in a broader sense. Because they are the point of balance between security and liberty, a decline in security causes the balance to shift against liberty. An even more basic point is that without physical security there is likely to be very little liberty. Who would dare, without protection against terrorist retaliation, to criticize Islam? Intimidation can stifle liberty as effectively as laws can.

More important than the one-sidedness of the civil libertarians' historical narrative is their assumption that the past is a good guide to the future (though they are not consistent in so assuming: if they were, they would not worry that the current national security measures may outlive the emergency that has called them forth). The past does not include attacks on the United States by terrorists wielding nuclear bombs, dirty bombs, biological weapons capable of killing millions of people, or other weapons of mass destruction; the future may well include such attacks. We must not emulate the Bourbon kings, who learned nothing and forgot nothing. Or, as another saying goes, if we want things to stay the same, things will have to change. Those who believe that since we survived decades of confrontation with the Soviet Union unscathed we have nothing to fear from a handful of terrorists are looking backward rather than forward. They are also being inconsistent, for they consider the post-9/11 security measures particularly ominous because the struggle against terrorism may never end. The Cold War showed no signs of ending either, till it ended, more than forty years after it had begun; our liberties survived. The fact that a struggle is protracted is no reason to suspend security measures before it ends; as long as we are threatened, we must defend.

Nixon's abuse of civil liberties, which civil libertarians believe is being repeated by President Bush (a belief sustained not by evidence but by liberals' visceral dislike of Bush), like our success in the Cold War, was also a product of historical conditions that no longer obtain. Violent protests against the Vietnam War, protests that took place against the background of a global struggle with communism and a surge of violent radical movements in the United States and other Western nations, caused law enforcement and intelligence agencies to become hypervigilant about possible subversive activities. In contrast, there is virtually no domestic opposition to the struggle against modern terrorism. This is in part because modern terrorism is more dangerous to the nation than the radical protests, agitation, and even violence of the Vietnam War era, and in part because the terrorists' ideology, unlike that of the earlier radicals, has as yet no significant domestic following.

In 2001, just months before the 9/11 attacks, my court, in our second *Alliance to End Repression* opinion (see Further Readings at the end of the book), ordered that a consent decree that had been entered in 1981, restricting the authority of the Chicago police department to investigate terrorist activity, be modified. The decree forbade investigations for any purpose other than obtaining evidence of past, present, or impending criminal conduct; forbade the collection of information about any political group to which the target of an investigation belonged or about its members or attendants at its meetings; and tightly limited the use of undercover informants and the gathering of information at rallies or other public assemblies of advocates of violence and other political extremists. The decree had been a response to violations of civil liberties committed by the police department's "Red Squad" in the 1960s and 1970s. In words eerily prophetic of the situation the nation finds itself in as a consequence of what the 9/11 attacks revealed about the nature of modern terrorism and the nation's vulnerability to it, we said:

> The era in which the Red Squad flourished is history, along with the Red Squad itself. The instabilities of that era have largely disappeared. Fear of communist subversion, so strong a motivator of constitutional infringements in those days, has disappeared along with the Soviet Union and the Cold War. Legal controls

over the police, legal sanctions for the infringement of constitutional rights, have multiplied. The culture that created and nourished the Red Squad has evaporated. The consent decree has done its job. . . . The City wants flexibility to meet new threats to the safety of Chicago's citizens. In the heyday of the Red Squad, law enforcers from J. Edgar Hoover's FBI on down to the local level in Chicago focused to an unhealthy degree on political dissidents, whose primary activity was advocacy though it sometimes spilled over into violence. Today the concern, prudent and not paranoid, is with ideologically motivated terrorism. The City does not want to resurrect the Red Squad. It wants to be able to keep tabs on incipient terrorist groups. New groups of political extremists, believers in and advocates of violence, form daily around the world. If one forms in or migrates to Chicago, the decree renders the police helpless to do anything to protect the public against the day when the group decides to commit a terrorist act. Until the group goes beyond the advocacy of violence and begins preparatory actions that might create reasonable suspicion of imminent criminal activity, the hands of the police are tied. And if the police have been forbidden to investigate until then, if the investigation cannot begin until the group is well on its way toward the commission of terrorist acts, the investigation may come too late to prevent the acts or to identify the perpetrators. If police get wind that a group of people have begun meeting and discussing the desirability of committing acts of violence in pursuit of an ideological agenda, a due regard for the public safety counsels allowing the police department to monitor the statements of the group's members, to build a file, perhaps to plant an undercover agent. All this the First Amendment permits (unless the motives of the police are improper or the methods forbidden by the Fourth Amendment or other provisions of federal or state law) but the decree forbids. The decree impedes efforts by the police to cope with the problems of today because earlier generations of police coped improperly with the problems of yesterday.

Civil libertarians are right to be concerned about the personal costs and potential political consequences of national security measures. A number of harmless members of the Communist Party lost their jobs during the McCarthy period, and serious errors of foreign policy may have resulted from Democrats' fear of being thought "soft on communism," such as our delay in exploiting the split between the Soviet Union and Red China and our overinvestment in trying to save South Vietnam from communist aggression. The post-9/11 sweeps that I mentioned caught a number of innocent fish in their nets, perhaps avoidably, to the detriment of good relations between the intelligence services and the American Muslim community. The more than 100,000 Japanese residents of the United States, a majority of them U.S. citizens, who were interned during World War II on groundless suspicion of their loyalty were innocent victims of a wartime measure that had racist and exploitative overtones.

But this is just to say that curtailing civil liberties imposes costs. As even (or perhaps especially) conservatives should realize, government initiatives in national security tend to be clumsy, costly, and deformed by politics—just like the government's social and economic initiatives, as in the many wasteful programs of the New Deal and Great Society. And sometimes the costs take the form of diminished national security: the FBI's heavy-handed measures against members of the U.S. Muslim community in the wake of the 9/11 attacks may have retarded our struggle against Islamist terrorism by alienating some members of a community whose loyalty is essential to the nation's security.

But the relevant question is not whether curtailing civil liberties imposes costs, to which the answer is obvious; it is whether the costs exceed the benefits. Civil libertarians tend to exaggerate the costs (how many innocent U.S. citizens in a population of 300 million have experienced real hardship as a result of the post-9/11 security measures?) and to ignore or slight the benefits. Most civil libertarians, and almost all their leaders, are lawyers. They are comfortable defending liberties recognized by law but uncomfortable assessing threats to national security, about which they know little and don't want to learn more. Liberty, they think, is part of law, is something therefore within their ken; national security is not. That is why, rather than becoming national security mavens, civil liberties lawyers are content to narrate a history of civil liberties violations.

I noted in passing the tiny conservative civil liberties movement, typified by the Cato Institute. A far more important movement within conservatism—call it "rights fundamentalism"—exercises a far greater check on national security measures. Put to one side those who read the Second Amendment literally and conclude that the government has no power to control private gun ownership, at least by law-abiding citizens; guns are unlikely to be the weapon of choice of terrorists operating in the United States. Far more dangerous is the resistance of business, in the name of property rights and free markets, to measures for regulating the safety of businesses that could become unwitting tools of terrorism. The airlines before 9/11 are a case in point. A current example is the chemical industry, which has fought tooth and nail, thus far successfully, against imposition of strict federal safety requirements designed to prevent chemicals from being used as weapons of mass destruction activated by attacks on plants in which toxic chemicals are stored and on shipments of toxic chemicals by rail or truck. Property rights can block national security measures as mischievously as rights of liberty and privacy can.

CHAPTER THREE

Rights Against Detention

I TURN NOW TO THE SPECIFIC constitutional rights that may be imperiled by measures to protect national security in times of emergency, that is, when the safety of the nation is believed to be unusually endangered. That is the reigning belief today because of the rise of global terrorism and the intertwined menace of weapons of mass destruction.

This chapter and the next take up the constitutional rights of individuals whom the federal government places in custody. (I shall generally disregard actions of state and local governments, which play a subordinate role in national security matters, though I did mention Chicago's "Red Squad" in the last chapter.) Suppose that a person suspected of being a terrorist is detained. If he is charged with a crime, a familiar set of rights (see below) is triggered. But suppose that, as is both common in counterterrorism and problematic, he isn't charged with a crime. What then? Here constitutional analysis begins with the right of habeas corpus. The Constitution presupposes rather than defines this right (just as it presupposes capital punishment by forbidding the government to deprive a person of his life without due process of law, and just as it presupposes judicial power to invalidate constitutional laws by making the Constitution a part of the "supreme Law of the Land"); it does this by providing that Congress may suspend habeas corpus only in times of rebellion or invasion. But the contours of the right of habeas corpus were well understood when the Constitution was written: the detained individual could compel his custodian to justify the detention to a judge. In the words of Blackstone, "if a probable ground be shewn, that the party is imprisoned without just cause, and therefore hath a right to be delivered, the writ of *habeas corpus* is then a writ of right, which 'may not be denied, but ought to be granted to every man that is committed, or detained in prison, or otherwise restrained, though it be by the command of the king, the privy council, or any other.'"

Congressional statutes, and judicial interpretations of them, have expanded the common-law right of habeas corpus to the point where it is now mainly a procedural mechanism by which prison inmates obtain federal post-appellate judicial review of the constitutionality of their convictions or sentences. I am concerned only with the constitutional minimum right of habeas corpus and not its statutory elaborations. From the constitutional standpoint, a showing that the prisoner is in prison pursuant to the judgment of a court of competent jurisdiction is probably sufficient to justify holding him. Historically (not that history is normative in the approach I take to constitutional law), habeas corpus was not a procedure for reexamining the findings made by a previous tribunal. But that is an aside; my concern is not with the use of habeas corpus in the criminal process but with its use as a vehicle by which people detained outside that process can challenge their detainment.

The constitutional right of habeas corpus, we should note before beginning to explore its substantive content, is not a right just of U.S. citizens. It may seem strange that the framers of the Constitution should have wanted noncitizens to have any constitutional rights.

But in the eighteenth century even more than now the United States was a nation of immigrants, and immigrants are not entitled to obtain citizenship the day they arrive in this country. The Naturalization Act of 1795 required that they live here for five years before they could gain citizenship, and this continues to be the law, though there are some exceptions. It would be difficult to attract immigrants, or for that matter tourists and other visitors, if they had no legal rights when they were in this country.

This is not to say that the constitutional rights of noncitizens are identical to those of citizens. For example, only a citizen can be president or a member of Congress; only a citizen has a constitutional right to vote or to bear arms; section 1 of the Fourteenth Amendment forbids states to abridge the privileges or immunities only of citizens; and it is an unsettled question whether aliens have rights under the First or Fourth Amendments. Moreover, it would not be constitutional to deport (now called "remove") a citizen, although a citizen can subject himself to deportation ("removal") by renouncing U.S. citizenship. And because deportation is a civil proceeding, the alien in a deportation proceeding does not enjoy the rights of a criminal defendant. Indeed, these proceedings are conducted by executive-branch officers rather than by judges. But as the Supreme Court reaffirmed in 2001 in a case called *Zadvydas v. Davis*, anyone who finds himself in the United States, unless he is an illegal entrant stopped at a port of entry, has *some* constitutional rights beyond the bare right to apply for habeas corpus. (The bare right might be nothing more than the right to insist on a showing that he is being detained by order of an official who has jurisdiction, whether or not properly exercised, to detain people on the ground on which the petitioner for habeas corpus has been detained.) In particular, he has the right to due process of law and the other rights, mainly of criminal defendants, conferred by the Fifth and Sixth Amendments; but remember that my particular concern is the rights of persons detained outside the criminal process.

So habeas corpus is not only a constitutional right in itself but also a vehicle for litigating other constitutional rights of detainees. The scope of a detainee's rights, however, depends on why he is being detained. If he is being detained as a material witness, his situation will be similar to that of a criminal defendant detained awaiting trial. If he is an alien who is ordered deported but whom no nation will accept, normally he cannot be kept in custody in the United States for more than six months (as the Court ruled in *Zadvydas*)—unless he is a suspected terrorist, in which event he can probably be detained indefinitely without violation of the Constitution.

The situation of a person who is being prosecuted for a crime is different from that of a material witness or of an alien facing removal proceedings. A criminal defendant has a long list of constitutional rights. They include a right to effective assistance of counsel (paid for by the government if he cannot afford to hire a lawyer), a right to a speedy trial, a right not to be tried twice for the same offense, a right to minimally decent jail conditions if he was not admitted to bail (to which he would also have a right, though a qualified one), a right to insist that his guilt be proved beyond a reasonable doubt, a right not to be incriminated by a coerced statement that he made in or out of court, a right not to be convicted for violating a statute that is hopelessly vague or was enacted after he violated it, a right to trial by jury (if the offense he is charged with is a felony) presided over, if he is a federal defendant, by a judge appointed in conformity with the requirements of Article III of the Constitution (therefore a judge appointed for life by the president, confirmed by the Senate, and removable only by impeachment by the House of Representatives and conviction by the Senate), and a right, if convicted, not to be subjected to any cruel and unusual punishments. If convicted and imprisoned, he will have limited First Amendment rights in prison and even a limited constitutional right to marry.

Rights not to be mistreated in prison are also enjoyed by persons detained for reasons other than criminal prosecution, such as material witnesses, persons imprisoned for civil contempt or awaiting deportation, or those committed by reason of insanity. And all detainees other than some prisoners of war, discussed next, and foreigners detained abroad have a right to the rudiments of due process of law, namely, a right to notice of the reason for their detention and an opportunity for a hearing to determine the legal and factual sufficiency of the reason. But that may be all.

The most obvious departure in the national security setting from the pattern of constitutional rights that I have described concerns prisoners of war. They have rights under international law, including rights conferred by international conventions to which the United States is a party. But if they are charged with being unlawful combatants, that is, with having violated the laws of war—for example by mistreating prisoners or by engaging in espionage or sabotage without wearing a uniform to identify them as enemy soldiers—they can be prosecuted before military tribunals and in this and other respects denied most of the constitutional rights of a criminal defendant. If they are foreigners being held outside the United States, they cannot even seek habeas corpus, as the Supreme Court held in *Johnson v. Eisentrager* (1950). On the other hand, prisoners of war may not lawfully be prosecuted merely for having fought or even killed Americans in combat, or be treated inhumanely, or be forced to reveal information beyond name, rank, and serial number. But these, to repeat, are not constitutional rights.

Terrorism on the scale of al-Qaeda's campaign of terrorism presents a challenge to this conventional picture of constitutional rights and their limitations. Suppose that in the U.S. invasion of Afghanistan in the fall of 2001, our soldiers capture in combat an al-Qaeda fighter who is not a U.S. citizen, and they intern him in a military base in Afghanistan, or perhaps in some other foreign nation. They grant him none of the rights that a prisoner of war has or that an ordinary criminal suspect in the United States would have; perhaps they even torture him for information. This conduct may violate rights that he has by virtue of international law or even U.S. domestic law, but it probably would not violate his constitutional rights. The Supreme Court's decision in *United States v. Verdugo-Urquidez* (1990) strongly suggests that he doesn't have any, although the holding was limited to the Fourth Amendment. U.S. laws, including the provisions of the Constitution, generally do not apply outside the United States. Congress can confer rights on foreigners with respect to conduct outside the United States if it wants to, but these would be statutory rights.

But we must consider two variants of this hypothetical case: the first where the action taken by our government is against a U.S. citizen and the second where a foreigner is interned on U.S. territory. The Constitution follows a citizen on his travels or sojourns outside the United States. So if our government seized a U.S. citizen abroad and tortured him, it could not defend its action by claiming that the Constitution has no extraterritorial application. The situation of the foreigner detained in the United States is more complicated. From the fact that a noncitizen who is residing, even if temporarily, in the United States has some constitutional rights, it does not follow that a foreigner seized abroad and brought to the United States does. Were he detained abroad he would not, and why should it make a difference that the government decides to intern him in the United States? From a practical standpoint the place of seizure is much more relevant than the place of detention to determining his rights. Yet the Supreme Court once held that a Japanese general who had been tried before a military tribunal on U.S. territory as a war criminal and was being held on U.S. territory following his conviction could seek habeas corpus (*In re Yamashita* [1946]).

Were it not for the *Yamashita* decision, the government would have had no reason to think it had anything to gain by interning suspected terrorists captured in Afghanistan or elsewhere abroad in the U.S. military prison at Guantánamo Bay, Cuba, rather than in the United States, on the theory that our military base there is not in the United States. It is not, but it is leased from Cuba in perpetuity, making it the practical equivalent of a U.S. territory, and in *Rasul v. Bush* (2004) the Supreme Court held, in a ruling consistent with *Yamashita*, that foreign persons detained there can seek habeas corpus.

Rasul seems like a sensible, "practical" decision, but may not be. Not because Guantánamo Bay is *really* in Cuba—there is no "really" in the matter—but because the decision may just encourage the government to hold more detainees abroad, say, in Afghanistan or Iraq, which no one supposes is U.S. territory; and what would be gained by that?

If the detainee is a U.S. citizen, his constitutional rights are unaffected by where he is being held. But what exactly are those rights? Might the unique character of modern terrorism justify a curtailment of the rights of the U.S. citizen captured fighting the United States in Afghanistan, or for that matter captured in the United States while planning a terrorist attack on behalf of al-Qaeda? Might it justify denying him the right to seek habeas corpus, thus allowing the government to detain him indefinitely, incommunicado, and without lodging any criminal charges against him? The argument would be that we are at war with al-Qaeda (we'll see later that there is a plausible basis for this characterization), so that a member of al-Qaeda, if we succeed in capturing him, is a prisoner of war. A prisoner of war has no greater rights by virtue of his being a U.S. citizen, as the Supreme Court held in *Ex parte Quirin* (1942).

This argument does not carry the government as far as it wants to go, however. The government doesn't want to give terrorists the rights of prisoners of war, which include most critically a right not to be forced to give information to their captors. So it adds that terrorists, because they do not obey the laws of war, are war criminals ("unlawful combatants," like the petitioners in *Quirin*) and so don't have all the rights of prisoners of war. Their only rights are those conferred by the international laws of war and the Uniform Code of Military Justice on unlawful combatants. As long as they are foreigners held abroad and thus cannot avail themselves of the *Yamashita* ruling, they cannot maintain an action for habeas corpus. But what if they are U.S. citizens, or foreigners captured and held in the United States? The government argues that a prisoner of war, whatever his nationality and wherever he is captured or detained, has no constitutional rights, not even the right of habeas corpus, and if he is an unlawful combatant he lacks most of the rights of a prisoner of war as well.

But General Yamashita was allowed to seek habeas corpus in order to get a judicial determination of whether he really was a war criminal, and it would be odd to deny the same right to a U.S. citizen, even one captured and held abroad, since the Constitution follows citizens wherever they go. But oddity to one side, there is a practical reason for thinking that the balance between security and liberty leans toward entitling such a person to seek habeas corpus. There is much greater uncertainty about membership in al-Qaeda than about membership in a conventional military formation. The danger of erroneously identifying an individual as an enemy of the United States is therefore much greater than in a conventional war. This difference weighs in favor of allowing him to obtain, by means of habeas corpus, judicial review of the grounds of his detention. National security would not be compromised significantly by requiring a judicial determination that the government had a justification for detaining him; what might count as a justification is no part of habeas corpus.

That the balance favors the right of habeas corpus is a judgment that is within the capacity of generalist judges—judges who are not specialists in national security—to make. The risk of a false positive (that is, of detaining an innocent person) is great and the cost of such a false positive (indefinite detention) also great. The government interest, in comparison, is slight. There is always the risk that a federal district judge, seconded by the court of appeals, will make a mistake and release a terrorist thinking him innocent (the false negative). But this risk can be minimized by placing a heavy burden on the detainee to prove that he is not a terrorist. It is because burdens of proof can be adjusted that the mere granting of the right to seek habeas corpus, without specifying the content of the habeas corpus proceeding, neither endangers national security nor imposes significant costs on the judicial system.

National security hawks might argue that there is no need for judicial review of detention decisions because the government has no more interest than judges do in detaining innocent people. True, but people whose profession is to protect national security are unlikely to give a great deal of weight to civil liberties unless required to do so by some outside force, such as the judiciary. They will be mindful of the costs to them of detaining innocent people and of the risk of alienating communities whose members they wish to conciliate, but they are unlikely to give much weight to the costs to the innocent detainees themselves.

The Supreme Court held in *Rasul v. Bush* that an individual who is detained on suspicion of being a terrorist (including a foreigner, if detained on U.S. territory, which for this purpose includes Guantánamo Bay) is indeed entitled to seek habeas corpus. If this is correct, as I believe it is, the government should not be allowed to thwart his right by the facile expedient of interning him abroad. The *Rasul* decision was based, however, on the federal habeas corpus statute rather than on the Constitution. A more important decision from a constitutional standpoint is *Hamdi v. Rumsfeld* (also 2004). Though unable to stitch together a majority opinion, the Court did make clear that due process entitles a U.S. citizen detained as an enemy combatant to require, by means of habeas corpus, that the factual basis for his detention be reviewed by a neutral decision maker. The Court did not discuss the status of a foreigner detained in the United States. But if the foreigner is a suspected terrorist, as distinct from a member of a military formation, and he was captured in the United States, he should have the same right as a citizen to a judicial determination of whether he really is a terrorist rather than a victim of mistaken identity. Otherwise foreigners visiting the United States will be outlaws in the literal sense of having no legal protections.

How much process a detainee suspected of being a terrorist can be given without endangering national security depends on such details as the timing of the habeas corpus proceeding. When should the right to seek habeas corpus be thought to arise? Immediately upon detention? Any delay beyond the short one (normally no more than forty-eight hours) required to take the suspect to a jail or to some other place of detention, process him, and give him a probable-cause hearing before a judicial officer will mean that the suspect is being held without a prompt judicial determination that there is an adequate reason to detain him. Is this a suspension of habeas corpus, therefore requiring congressional action based upon a finding that the nation is in the throes of rebellion or invasion? Is it consistent with the right not to be deprived of one's liberty without due process of law?

The answers would be obvious (yes and no, respectively) in the ordinary criminal context. The terrorist context complicates the analysis. The government may have a compelling reason to hold a suspected terrorist incommunicado for more than forty-eight hours:

namely, to avoid tipping off his accomplices that the government has seized him, while meanwhile extracting from him information that it can use to arrest them before their suspicions are aroused, or even to "turn" him so that he becomes a double agent, spying on his erstwhile accomplices. Recruiting a double agent tends to be a protracted process and one that for obvious reasons must be conducted in secret. Holding a terrorist suspect incommunicado also facilitates forms of coercive interrogation that do not quite cross the line that separates accepted interrogation tactics from torture (discussed in the next chapter). A detainee who feels isolated and has no access to a lawyer can more easily be pressured to provide information sought by the government. The principal argument for torture is that it works quickly; the substitute methods of interrogation may take much longer to elicit the desired information and so their successful employment may require protracted detention of the suspect—in secret.

These concerns have sufficient weight, given the gravity of the terrorist threat, the brevity and vagueness of the constitutional text (which does not explain what "suspending" habeas corpus means, let alone define "due process of law"), the tradition of loose interpretation of that text, and the limitations of judicial knowledge of national security needs, to justify interpreting the suspension clause to permit the detention of a terrorist suspect incommunicado for a reasonable time without supposing that by doing this the right of habeas corpus has been suspended. But I repeat a caveat from the Introduction: special rules for terrorism are warranted only for terrorism that potentially threatens national security. "Ecoterrorism" and "animal rights terrorism" do not. These are serious crimes, but they inflict only property damage, usually modest, and are orders of magnitude less menacing than Islamist terrorism. Of course this may change; the Unabomber was a proto-ecoterrorist, and a biological Unabomber could be a greater menace than al-Qaeda. The important thing is to avoid leaping to the conclusion that all politically motivated crime is sufficiently dangerous to imperil national security.

How long it is "reasonable" to hold a suspected terrorist incommunicado cannot be specified in advance. It depends on the answers to such questions as how likely it is that protracted detention would yield significant benefits for national security in the form of additional arrests or of a more complete detection, penetration, and disruption of terrorist activities or preparations. All that is clear is that the longer the period of detention, the greater the hardship to the person detained (who may after all be innocent) and the less likely it is that further detention would yield significant information or other benefits. The benefits diminish with time and the costs increase with time; when the curves cross, the detainee should be brought before a judicial officer for a determination of whether further detention is necessary. Continued detention beyond that point without judicial review would constitute a suspension of habeas corpus. Congress has not authorized that, and it is doubtful whether it could do so in the present situation. For it would be a stretch to characterize the situation as one of actual or impending "invasion" by our terrorist enemies, though there may be terrorist sleeper cells in the United States and we do not know when and where terrorists will strike next.

The next question is how much proof an individual detained as a terrorist should be allowed to demand of the government. The answer requires balancing the costs of false positives against those of false negatives. The less proof the judge requires that an individual really is a terrorist, the greater the number of harmless people who will be mistakenly interned. The more proof the judge requires, the greater the number of terrorists who will mistakenly be released. Requiring proof beyond a reasonable doubt in criminal cases causes many guilty defendants to be acquitted and many other guilty persons not to be charged in the first place. We accept this as a price worth paying to protect the innocent. But ordinary crime does not imperil national security; modern terrorism does, so the government's burden of proof should be lighter, though how much lighter is a matter of judgment.

The government might be reluctant to disclose publicly its evidence (however much or little was required) that the detainee was a terrorist lest it reveal valuable information to the terrorists still at large. This problem could be solved by allowing the evidence to be presented to the judge *in camera*, that is, without being made public or even disclosed to the applicant for habeas corpus (or to his lawyer, if he has one). An intermediate solution would be to allow disclosure only to the lawyer, provided that he qualified for a security clearance.

It is true that the Constitution entitles a criminal defendant to a public trial. A trial can be public even if not all the evidence is public; evidence is often placed under seal if making it public would disclose a trade secret or gratuitously embarrass a witness or a party. But the evidence is available to the parties; it is impossible to defend a case when you're not told what the evidence of your guilt is. However, a person detained under the suggested approach would not be a criminal defendant. That is a vital qualification because it is unclear how in a criminal trial, where the defendant has a constitutional right to be tried by a jury and to confront the witnesses for the prosecution, national security secrets could be adequately protected.

To summarize the chapter thus far, there is a persuasive argument for interpreting the Constitution to permit indefinite detention of U.S. citizens, limited to suspected terrorists and distinct from criminal punishment, without requiring proof beyond a reasonable doubt that the suspect really is a terrorist and without granting him most of the other rights of criminal defendants. All that should be required is a persuasive showing to a judge in an adversary hearing that the suspect really is a terrorist. His status would be similar though not identical to that of a prisoner of war, consistent with the similarities and dissimilarities of the "war on terrorism" to a conventional war.

Even the grant of these rather limited constitutional rights to the detained terrorist suspect might seem excessive, or, more precisely, redundant, on the theory I mentioned earlier that the government itself has an interest in separating the guilty from the innocent. It is costly to detain people, detaining the innocent can impair deterrence (in the limit, if detention is random, the threat of detention would have no deterrent effect), and it is bad public relations. But if the government could be trusted to give due weight to these considerations, we would not need judicially enforceable rights, or even Article III courts; adjudication could be left to tribunals created within the executive branch.

No explicit constitutional text or precedent blocks the suggested resolution of the dilemma of what to do with terrorist suspects. About all that can be said in general is that the greater the perceived terrorist menace, the greater will be, and should be, the judges' inclination to resolve doubts in favor of detention and its continuation unless and until the danger diminishes significantly. Assessing the relevant needs and dangers requires a weighing of imponderables. The subjectivity of the process, which I have acknowledged and indeed emphasized in the preceding chapters, is underscored by the etymology of "imponderable"; it comes from *ponderare*, Latin for "to weigh." To weigh the unweighable is at once a contradiction and an inescapable duty.

The suggested approach will not satisfy the legalistic thinker who believes that the only possible justifications for detention are crime and war and that war means a violent conflict with a foreign state, not with a private group however menacing. Someone mesmerized by this dichotomy is apt to conclude that a terrorist can be detained only as a criminal and as such should have all the rights that criminal defendants enjoy. But it is incorrect that the only grounds of detention are crime and war. A person can be detained as a lunatic dangerous to himself or others though he may never have committed a crime. This example, along with that of denial of bail to a defendant believed to be a flight risk, the restrictions placed on sexual predators after they have served their time, the imposition of a quarantine to prevent the spread of an epidemic, and the longer prison sentences given to criminals thought likely to recidivate than to other criminals, shows that there can be a purely preventive basis for limiting personal liberty. Some enemy combatants captured in the campaign in Afghanistan and detained at the U.S. military prison at Guantánamo Bay without criminal proceedings being instituted have been released only to be found later fighting the United States in Iraq or Afghanistan. If a judge is convinced that the individual detained is a terrorist, this should be enough to justify the individual's continued detention, much as if he were a prisoner of war.

Maybe he *is* a prisoner of war. For if we are at war with al-Qaeda, the national security "hawk" can give the civil libertarians their war/crime dichotomy and still come out ahead. Three days after the 9/11 attacks Congress issued a joint resolution (the AUMF—Authorization for Use of Military Force) authorizing the president "to use all necessary and appropriate force against those nations, organizations, or persons he determines planned, authorized, committed, or aided the terrorist attacks that occurred on September 11, 2001, or harbored such organizations or persons, in order to prevent any future acts of international terrorism against the United States by such nations, organizations or persons." The AUMF supplies the minor premise of the following syllogism advanced by John Yoo: by making the president the commander in chief of the armed forces, Article II of the Constitution authorizes him to conduct war in any manner he sees fit; we are at war with al-Qaeda; therefore it is the sole prerogative of the president to decide what if any rights to accord to persons captured in this war.

That is an extravagant interpretation of presidential authority. It confuses commanding the armed forces with exercising dictatorial control over the waging of war, the kind of control exercised by a Napoleon or a Hitler or a Stalin, or by dictators in the Roman Republic, who were appointed by the Roman Senate for six-month terms during national emergencies. The confusion is apparent from the fact that the president is commander in chief in peacetime as well as in wartime. Does Yoo believe that in peacetime the president can, for example, institute conscription without congressional authorization? If he can do it in wartime, it is not by virtue of his being commander in chief but by virtue of his being authorized elsewhere in the Constitution to assume dictatorial powers in wartime. But there is no elsewhere, as the Supreme Court made clear in *Youngstown Sheet & Tube Co. v. Sawyer*, where it held that President Truman could not seize the nation's steel industry during the Korean War even to prevent a possible interruption of military supplies. Without making clear whether he agrees with *Youngstown*, Yoo argues that Congress's control of the purse strings creates an adequate check on the president's abusing his plenary powers to conduct war. But that is a contradiction. If the powers are truly plenary, the president can seize whatever assets or properties he needs in order to finance the war—beginning with the steel industry.

Moreover, the existence of a power need not extinguish all rights with which the power collides. It does not follow that Congress, because Article I of the Constitution authorizes it to regulate foreign and domestic commerce, can pass a law forbidding the shipment across state lines of magazines that criticize Congress, or can require that anyone convicted of hijacking a truck in interstate commerce be drawn and quartered. The powers that the Constitution grants to Congress and the president have to be adjusted to the rights that the Constitution grants the individuals affected by exertions of those powers. The Third Amendment forbids the quartering of soldiers in private homes in time of peace, or in time of war otherwise than "in a manner prescribed by law." That is an express limitation on the president's authority as commander in chief; an implicit limitation is the grant of authority to Congress, but not to the president, to suspend habeas corpus in the case of an invasion of the United States. Article I confers a variety of war-related powers on Congress, including the power "to make Rules for the Government and Regulation of the land and naval Forces." The *Hamdi* decision treats the AUMF as a declaration of war authorizing the detention of enemy combatants, yet still accords them, at least if they are citizens, the constitutional right of due process.

But when a power collides with a right, it is not necessarily the power that must give way. The Bill of Rights was adopted after the power-conferring provisions of the Constitution, but that does not require that it be interpreted as having repealed those provisions, gravely weakening the nation, or otherwise as having profoundly altered the structure of government that the original document had created. Suppose the survival of the nation in wartime depended on an immediate quartering of troops in people's homes but no law authorizing that quartering had been enacted; it would be arguable that the president had implicit authority, as commander in chief of the armed forces in a desperate war, to override the Third Amendment. Similarly, in its recent decision in *Rumsfeld v. FAIR* (2006), the Supreme Court implied that the grant of national defense powers to Congress in Article I can affect the scope of First Amendment rights, even though Article I, a part of the Constitution of 1787, preceded the First Amendment. It is uncontroversial that as commander in chief the president can impose *some* restrictions on what would ordinarily be constitutional rights, because military discipline requires that soldiers give up many of the rights they enjoy as private citizens. Moreover, as in the case of quartering troops in time of war, if necessary without an authorizing statute, the president can impose more restrictions in war than in peace because a commander in chief's responsibilities are different and broader in war.

If he can go even further and impose a Roman-style dictatorship, the more effectively to prosecute a war, this would be not because he is commander in chief but because of the urgent necessities of a desperate situation. The authority to respond to those necessities might be thought implicitly granted the president by the Constitution. The Supreme Court thought this true of the president's furnishing a bodyguard to a Supreme Court justice when it said in 1890 in *Cunningham v. Neagle* (paradoxically a habeas corpus case, brought by the bodyguard) that the president's constitutional duty to "take care that the laws be faithfully executed" is not "limited to the enforcement of acts of congress or of treaties of the United States according to their express terms," but "includes the rights, duties, and obligations growing out of the constitution itself, our international relations, and all the protection implied by the nature of the government under the constitution." The authority might even be thought extraconstitutional—the *Curtiss-Wright* principle mentioned in the Introduction. As Martin Sheffer puts it, "during an emergency the law of necessity supersedes the law of the Constitution."

Even apart from the "law of necessity," there are limits to Congress's authority to interfere with the presidential conduct of a war. Congress could not require the president to submit his battle plans to it for approval; that would be usurping his constitutional prerogative as commander in chief. Or suppose, to take a more timely example, that the United States was invaded by a foreign power and the president ordered the National Security Agency to intercept the invading force's electronic communications without complying with the requirements of the Foreign Intelligence Surveillance Act. It would be doubtful (I would say more than doubtful) that Congress could deny the president the authority enjoyed by any commander in chief to collect signals intelligence in a war; more on this in the next chapter.

The *Youngstown* decision is consistent with this understanding of presidential authority. The Constitution gives the president the command of the armed forces, but it gives Congress the responsibility for maintaining them and hence for supplying them. It was the threatened interruption of supply that President Truman sought to prevent by his action in seizing the steel mills. It would have been a different case had Congress commanded Truman to move the First Marine Division from one position on the battlefront to another or to delay the Inchon landing by a week. That would have been congressional interference with Truman's constitutional authority as commander in chief.

The difficult case is where Congress's Article I authority to make "Rules for the Government and Regulation of the land and naval Forces" overlaps the president's Article II operational authority. A law forbidding the armed forces to torture prisoners would be a rule for "Government and Regulation," but a presidential directive to use torture in a desperate war would be a tactical military order.

SHORTLY AFTER THE 9/11 ATTACKS, the Department of Defense established "military commissions" to try suspected terrorists. These commissions are in effect specialized administrative courts. Military officers preside, there is no jury, the trial can be closed to the public, and the rules of evidence are relaxed—any probative evidence can be admitted, regardless of how obtained. The government wants to punish the worst of our terrorist enemies as war criminals. But unless they are U.S. citizens (who are not subject to the order creating the military tribunals) it does not want to try them in an ordinary criminal court, where it might have to reveal sensitive information in order to obtain a conviction, where certain evidence, though reliable, could not be presented, and where the terrorist defendants would have a public platform for denouncing the United States and rallying supporters. Soldiers captured in a war who are believed to have committed war crimes can lawfully be tried by military tribunals rather than by the ordinary courts.

To argue that the "war on terrorism" isn't *really* a war is not an adequate response to the administration's argument for trial by military tribunal. It is not a war in the sense that World War II was a war. But we talk about the "war in Iraq" even though the "insurgents," as they are usually called, use almost exclusively the methods of terrorists and do not constitute an organized state or even a shadow state (they appear to have no central command structure). The Authorization for Use of Military Force is tantamount to a declaration of war, though not against all terrorist groups, just against al-Qaeda and its affiliates. But Congress's power to suspend peacetime liberties even by an express declaration of war cannot be unbounded. It could not suspend the constitutional rights of suspected pickpockets by declaring war against pickpockets, or of gangsters by declaring war on the Mafia.

As with so many legal dichotomies, that of "crime" versus "war" does not fit an emergent reality, in this case that of global terrorism. It is an occupational hazard of lawyers to stall in their consideration of issues at the semantic level. Rather than ask whether modern terrorism is more like crime or more like war and therefore which box it should be put in, one should ask why there are different legal regimes for crime and war and let the answer guide the design of a sensible regime for fighting terrorism. It is not war as such but the dangers created by war that explain and justify a curtailment of civil liberties in the waging of war. A similar curtailment may be justified by the dangers posed by terrorists avid to acquire weapons of mass destruction. The constitutionality of subjecting terrorist suspects to trial by military tribunal ought to depend not on whether the "war against terrorism" is *really* a war (and there is no "really," since one is speaking of definitions, and definitions are mutable) but rather on whether there is a strong enough national security interest in so proceeding to overcome the prudent reluctance to enlarge the wartime powers of the president and Congress by expanding the conventional definition of "war."

This is actually a liberating perspective, which the government might be wise to embrace. Instead of pretending that the Constitution makes the president a military dictator and trying to shoehorn the struggle against global terrorism into a box labeled "war" and debating over whom exactly Congress was declaring war on in the AUMF, the government would be pointing to facts that show that modern terrorism is so dangerous, and so unlike ordinary crime, that the ordinary processes of criminal justice must be modified. The terrorist problem is sui generis; so should be the solution to it.

But in deference to the concerns of civil libertarians we must ask just how maladapted to dealing with the terrorist menace is the ordinary criminal process. Criminal courts can seal sensitive evidence and can prevent defendants from disrupting proceedings by making irrelevant speeches or otherwise acting up in the courtroom, at the same time giving the defendant a neutral decision maker and a set of procedural protections, such as the right to the assistance of a lawyer and to trial by jury, that reduce the risk of erroneous convictions without greatly increasing the risk of erroneous acquittals. Despite appearances, the balance of advantages in a federal criminal trial lies with the government, especially in a case against an unpopular defendant, because the federal government has much greater resources for litigation than any defendant.

But this picture is too simple. Although a disruptive defendant can be ejected from the courtroom, a defendant who decides to represent himself—which is his constitutional right, according to the Supreme Court, though it is nowhere mentioned in the Constitution— can use the dual role of lawyer-client to turn the trial into a political circus. In addition, perfectly reliable evidence seized in violation of a defendant's Fourth or Fifth Amendment rights is inadmissible in court trials (except that the Fourth Amendment probably cannot be invoked by someone who is not a U.S. citizen or lawful permanent resident), and in some cases the exclusion of such evidence precludes the conviction of guilty people. There are other limitations on the admissibility of evidence as well, limitations designed to avoid confusing a jury or prejudicing it against the defendant—but there is no jury in a military trial. And I indicated earlier the difficulty of keeping national security secrets sealed in a courtroom setting, where the defendant has a right to demand a jury and to confront the witnesses against him. In short, criminal prosecutions of suspected terrorists could founder on procedural protections designed for ordinary criminals tried in ordinary courts.

But why *military* tribunals, if the objective is merely to tilt the playing field a bit more against the defendant? The most questionable feature of such a tribunal is precisely its military composition and the resulting appearance of captors' justice. It is only the desire to find a familiar pigeonhole for a truncated version of a standard criminal trial that makes recourse to a military tribunal an attractive option. Call the tribunal "military" if you wish, in obedience to the conventional thinking that considers "war" and "crime" to divide the world of violence between them; it need not follow that it must be staffed by military personnel. The judges of the Nuremberg tribunal that tried the Nazi leaders were civilians, though the tribunal was officially a military tribunal.

It remains to consider the relation between the right of habeas corpus and trial before a military tribunal. A detainee, subject to qualifications noted earlier, should have the right to insist that a regular court make the initial determination whether he can be held as a likely terrorist; if the court determines that he is, he can then be handed over to a military tribunal for trial as an unlawful combatant.

CHAPTER FOUR

Rights Against Brutal Interrogation, and Against Searches and Seizures

SUPPOSING THAT AN INTERNED SUSPECTED TERRORIST fails to gain his freedom through habeas corpus, we must consider what the government can do to him while he is detained, and specifically how forcefully it can interrogate him. The issue usually arises in the context of a prosecution rather than a detention, when the government tries to place in evidence the defendant's confession obtained in the interrogation and the defendant objects on the ground that the confession was coerced. Coerced confessions, even when corroborated, are made inadmissible in evidence by interpretation of the Fifth Amendment's self-incrimination clause, though "coerced" is somewhat loosely interpreted in this context. The courts allow the government to use a certain amount of trickery, and to make at least implied promises of lenity, in an effort to extract a confession. Custodial interrogation is, to a degree, inherently coercive, yet it is permitted; even protracted custodial interrogation is permitted. But the line is drawn well short of torture; lesser forms of coercion, such as the old "third degree" (bright lights), sleep deprivation, frightening threats, and the injection of truth serum, are forbidden.

Forbidden, that is, when the confession induced by such means is used as evidence. Suppose it is not, because the government has decided not to prosecute; or it is, but the defendant is acquitted; or it is used only to justify noncriminal detention. The first case (no prosecution) and the third (noncriminal detention) are common in the struggle against terrorism. The first is common because often it is more important to know what your enemy is up to than to keep him in custody—if you know his plans, you should be able to thwart them, while if you prosecute him you may be providing valuable information to his accomplices—and the third because of the problems with trials of terrorists that I discussed in the last chapter. Suppose that in any of the three cases the person interrogated sues his interrogators on the ground that they have violated his constitutional rights. Which rights? It cannot be the right not to be compelled to incriminate oneself, because if the confession is not used to convict one, one has not been incriminated. But the victim of brutal interrogation might appeal to the due process clause as interpreted by the Supreme Court in *Rochin v. California* (1952)

Police had Rochin's stomach pumped to recover two capsules of morphine that he had swallowed while they were trying to arrest him. The Court, in a pretentious and overwrought opinion by Justice Frankfurter, concluded

> that the proceedings by which this conviction was obtained do more than offend some fastidious squeamishness or private sentimentalism about combatting crime too energetically. This is conduct that shocks the conscience. Illegally breaking into the privacy of the petitioner, the struggle to open his mouth and remove what was there, the forcible extraction of his stomach's contents—this course of proceeding by agents of government to obtain evidence is bound to offend even hardened sensibilities.

They are methods too close to the rack and the screw to permit of constitutional differentiation.

What makes the case significant is precisely the remoteness of stomach pumping (it was done by a physician at a hospital) from the rack and screw, two standard medieval torture techniques. If stomach pumping is a deprivation of liberty without due process of law, even more clearly torture is, as well as lesser forms of coercive interrogation.

But *Rochin* is special in several respects. First, it involved a search rather than an interrogation, and a search that had produced evidence used to convict the person searched. The reason the search was analyzed under the due process clause, rather than under the Fourth Amendment's prohibition of unreasonable searches and seizures, was that the Court had not yet imposed the Fourth Amendment's exclusionary rule—the rule that excludes from evidence the fruits of an unconstitutional search—on the states. The Court held that the evidence obtained by means of the stomach pump should have been excluded from Rochin's criminal trial because it was the product of what the Court considered a particularly outrageous search. It is only by extension that *Rochin* is authority for the proposition that interrogations that shock the conscience violate the Constitution. But it is a natural extension. Because interrogations are not searches, the due process clause is the only basis for mounting a constitutional challenge to a brutal interrogation that does not produce evidence used in a criminal proceeding.

Second, although excluding illegally obtained evidence from a criminal prosecution is conventionally regarded as merely a remedy for the underlying illegality, one can think of a search for evidence as presenting a different kind of constitutional issue from a search unrelated to an interest in prosecution. The latter is the kind of search that intelligence officers (as distinct from police officers) conduct in quest of information that might enable them to foil a terrorist's plans or recruit him as a double agent. The interference with personal liberty is less when no prosecution is in view. This point is obscured when considering a physical search, as in *Rochin*, because such a search is intrusive and disruptive (in *Rochin*, probably even painful), even if it doesn't lead to a prosecution. The point is doubly obscured when torture is used in an interrogation. In contrast, in the case of wiretapping or other electronic surveillance there ordinarily is no trespass, no intrusion beyond that inherent in any eavesdropping. That the fruits of a covert surveillance might be used to prosecute the subject of the surveillance is the worst consequence that most people would anticipate from it; if that prospect is removed, the injury inflicted by the surveillance is attenuated. There is still an invasion of privacy, but the gravity of unobtrusive invasions of privacy tends to be exaggerated, as we shall see in Chapter 6. Even the harm of coercive interrogation, which is not unobtrusive, is at least mitigated when there is no prospect of prosecution.

Third, Rochin was suspected merely of a drug offense. He was not a terrorist who had swallowed the plan of an attack. The greater the potential value of the information sought to be elicited by an interrogation, the greater should be the amount of coercion deemed permitted by the Constitution. The Constitution contains no explicit prohibition of coercive interrogation, or even of torture, to block such an approach. The Eighth Amendment's prohibition of cruel and unusual punishments comes into play only after a criminal defendant is sentenced, and the Fifth Amendment's prohibition against compelled self-incrimination only when the government wants to use the information that it has extracted from a person to convict him of a crime. All that limits coerced interrogation not used to obtain evidence, as far as the Constitution is concerned, is the Supreme Court's interpretation in the *Rochin* case of the Fifth Amendment's prohibition against depriving a person of life, liberty, or property without due process of law.

The interpretive space created by the due process clause is vast, and *Rochin* narrows it only slightly. Detention deprives a person of liberty, clearly; if beating a person or pumping his stomach also does, then "liberty" bears a meaning of uncertain extension. Likewise, if "process" means more than procedure, exactly what more does it mean? What process is due a person who refuses to divulge information of utmost importance to the welfare of society? Can the "conscience-shocking" effect of a stomach pump be divorced from the circumstances in which government officers resort to that method of obtaining information, so that the greater the necessity of getting the information the less will forcible methods of getting it shock the conscience? All these are open questions.

The value of the information sought depends in part on the menace to social welfare that has motivated the interrogation. If it is dire enough and the value of the information great enough, only a diehard civil libertarian will deny the propriety of using a high degree of coercion to elicit the information. It might be the whereabouts of a kidnapping victim, the location of a ticking time bomb, the site of a biological weapon about to be deployed, the identity of key terrorist leaders, or the details of terrorist plots. The diehard will reply that the benefits of coercion in such cases would be illusory because coercive interrogation, even to the degree implied by the (vague) word *torture*, never works. That is incorrect. Quite apart from the abundant evidence that torture *is* often an effective method of eliciting true information, which is also the common sense of the situation, methods of coercive interrogation well short of torture but more coercive than is permissible for eliciting statements used in an ordinary criminal proceeding are often effective too. It is true that some people will not give truthful information even under torture and that most people who are tortured will babble out *something* even if they know nothing of what the investigators want, thus sending the investigators off on wild-goose chases. But this is just to identify another cost of torture—the many false positives that it produces. It is not to say that there never are net benefits.

Bear in mind, however, that the relevant benefits of torture are the *incremental* benefits: only the benefits that would *not* be obtained by methods of coercive interrogation short of torture should be compared with the (also incremental) costs of torture. Conceivably, those incremental benefits are zero or close to it except when there is real urgency to obtaining the information; torture is likely to succeed in eliciting information more quickly than milder methods. To be able to make a confident judgment about the benefits of coercion, therefore, we need systematic knowledge of the efficacy of different degrees of coercion in extracting information from recalcitrant suspects. Pending acquisition of such knowledge, the *Rochin*-based understanding that torture (whether of a U.S. citizen abroad or of any person in the United States) is unconstitutional may as a practical matter be unassailable. The negative connotations of the word *torture* are simply too great. Should they be?

We execute people, and though the execution itself is not very painful, the contemplation of one's impending execution must be psychological torture of the most exquisite kind. It seems odd, moreover, to regard the greater deprivation, death, as less objectionable than the lesser one, torture (ask yourself whether you'd rather be executed or tortured)—even when the person tortured has caused more harm than the person executed. In combat soldiers kill and maim without supposing that they are doing anything wrong.

The civil libertarian case against torture resembles the civil libertarian case against capital punishment in not being primarily instrumental. Civil libertarians generally emphasize the contribution that civil liberties make to protecting innocent people and bolstering democracy, but even if no innocent person were ever executed or tortured many civil libertarians would continue to condemn capital punishment and torture. The real ground for their condemnation is revulsion. The importance of revulsion as a factor in morality and law cannot be denied, but it should not be allowed to occlude consideration of instrumental considerations. The unreliability of evidence procured by torture (the problem of false positives) is a compelling practical reason for excluding such evidence from a criminal trial. But reliability is not the critical issue when torture is used to obtain national security intelligence.

The idea that torture is not only a cruel and ugly practice but just about the worst thing that a government can do confuses torture as a routine practice of dictators, often intended to intimidate rather than to elicit information, and as a method long used to extract false confessions to political crimes and (necessarily false) confessions to nonexistent crimes such as sorcery, with torture as an exceptional method of counterterrorist interrogation. It is especially odd to issue an unqualified condemnation of a practice that almost everyone (including Senator John McCain, the nation's preeminent opponent of torture) accepts the necessity of resorting to in extreme situations.

Public efforts at justifying torture are doomed in the present climate of opinion, however, and public they would have to be because the U.S. government seems at present incapable of keeping a secret for long. We cannot be certain of this, because we cannot exclude the possibility that the government has successfully concealed a number of important secrets from us; we do not know what we do not know. But any use of torture is almost certain to become public knowledge sooner or later (partly because there is widespread opposition to torture within the military and intelligence services), and probably sooner, accompanied by irrefutable photographic evidence, producing political costs in excess of any likely benefits. It thus is unlikely that the U.S. government would authorize torture except in an extreme emergency, especially torture done by Americans in the United States or of a U.S. citizen anywhere, unless it thought it could conceal it, and it would be mistaken to think it could. (The "rendition" of foreigners captured abroad to nations that may practice torture, though a rather transparent evasion of the torture taboo, arouses less indignation.)

This analysis places great weight on the exact meaning of *torture*. The term must not be defined so broadly that it prohibits all methods of coercion used in an investigation; the risk to national security would be too great. Unfortunately, the word lacks a stable definition. It is like the word *slavery*. Slavery is simply involuntary servitude of which we disapprove; we do not call prisoners forced to work in prison, children assigned chores by their parents or forced to repeat classes that they flunk, or army conscripts "slaves." *Torture* has a little more fixity; it is not simply the set of methods of coercive interrogation of which we disapprove. It would not be an abuse of language to say that we would approve of using torture to extract information about the location of a nuclear bomb set to explode in Washington, D.C. If you shove a knife under a person's fingernails to induce him to give information, you are torturing him even if, in the circumstances, torture is warranted to avert a greater evil.

The word's stable core of meaning is the infliction of severe pain or suffering, whether physical or mental, on a person in custody, nowadays usually though not always for the purpose of extracting information. This is the definition in the Convention Against Torture. The definition leaves plenty of room for nasty tactics of interrogation. But the convention itself may not, as is apparent from its full title: "Convention Against Torture and Other Cruel, Inhuman or Degrading Treatment or Punishment." So at one end of the interrogation spectrum we have torture, at the other end the kind of mildly coercive methods that the Supreme Court permits to be used to obtain statements for use in criminal proceedings, and in the middle "cruel, inhuman or degrading treatment" that doesn't reach the level of torture. As a signatory of the convention, the United States is committed (with certain reservations that I cannot pause to discuss) to refraining from such treatment as well. But committed as a matter of constitutional law, by virtue of *Rochin?* It may seem obvious that the answer is yes, since the use of a stomach pump by a physician in a hospital to extract evidence lies near the lower end of this middle category. But the answer becomes less obvious if we focus on what has come to be thought the key issue in a *Rochin* type of case: whether the method used shocks the conscience. For unlike a test that focuses on the amount of pain and suffering inflicted by a particular method of interrogation, *Rochin*'s test is a relative one. What shocks the conscience depends on circumstances. In life-and-death situations the use of even highly coercive methods of interrogation is unlikely to shock the conscience of most people, even thoughtful and humane ones.

Many consciences will not be shocked at the use of torture when it will ward off a great evil and no other method would work quickly enough to be effective. The question arises whether we should relax the prohibition against torture in such a case or trust public officers to perceive and act on a moral duty that is higher than their legal duty. I favor the latter course.

There is a long tradition of civil disobedience, and while the term is usually applied to private individuals who deem it their moral duty to disobey positive law, there is no reason why it cannot also be used of public officials who do the same thing. Lincoln was engaged in civil disobedience when he suspended habeas corpus during the Civil War on his own authority and when he defied an order by the chief justice of the United States granting habeas corpus to a Confederate sympathizer in the face of the suspension (*Ex parte Merryman* [1861]). But he was as right to disobey the law in his situation as Gandhi and Martin Luther King Jr. were right to do so in their situations. In the era of weapons of mass destruction, torture may sometimes be the only means of averting the death of thousands, even millions, of Americans. In such a situation it would be the moral and political duty of the president to authorize torture. It seems odd that people who accept this point nevertheless denounce torture with such ferocity.

Civil disobedience by public officials is closely related to the exercise of discretion not to prosecute a criminal. When a district attorney declines to prosecute a person who is in fact guilty of a crime, because the crime is minor and the prosecutor has a better use for his limited resources, he is refusing to enforce the law, and this could be considered a lawless act. But we think it better to grant him that discretionary authority than to try to specify in the law when he may decline to prosecute. Similarly, it is probably better to recognize the discretion of public officers to disregard in extreme cases the prohibition against torture, or the discretion of the president to suspend habeas corpus in such cases though not authorized by the Constitution to do so, than to try to codify the instances in which such conduct is allowed.

Codification would amount to authorizing executive officials to suspend all rights. There are three objections. The first is the impracticability of specifying the circumstances in which the suspension would be appropriate without creating negative implications that might handicap officials when the unexpected happened. The second objection, derived in part from the first, is that officials would be tempted to test the outer bounds of so extraordinary a grant of authority, and they would have fair prospects for pushing them outward because, as just indicated, the grant of authority could not be worded too precisely lest it leave an emergency situation unprovided for. This erosion of boundaries was the experience under the constitution of Germany's Weimar Republic, which authorized the president of the republic to suspend constitutional rights in emergency situations, paving the way for Hitler. And third, denying officials a safe harbor and thus forcing them to assume the legal and political risks of disobeying the law in order to exercise extraordinary power should act as a check (doubtless imperfect) on such exercise. They will be reluctant to act unless a powerful moral justification, overriding the infamy of a legal violation, can be advanced. Otherwise they would be courting prosecution or civil suits, and in the president's case impeachment.

I acknowledge the danger of bringing law into disrepute if violations are condoned, especially when the law violated is not unjust but merely too demanding in particular circumstances. In the present context, this is a compelling argument for defining torture extremely narrowly, so that necessary violations of the law against torture do not become routine.

I HAVE ASSUMED UP TO NOW, in both the previous chapter and this one, that a terrorist suspect has been captured on the field of battle. I have considered how he might challenge his detention on constitutional grounds and, if the challenge fails, how he might challenge brutal interrogation by his captors on such grounds. Now suppose instead that he was arrested in his apartment in New York City and the apartment was searched and valuable evidence of his terrorist activities or connections was found, or that his phone was tapped. Ordinarily an arrest and a search (and wiretapping and other electronic eavesdropping are now considered searches for Fourth Amendment purposes) are constitutional only if there is probable cause to believe that the person arrested has committed a crime and that the search will turn up contraband or evidence of crime. "Probable cause" is more than a hunch or mere suspicion, even reasonable suspicion, but less than proof sufficient for conviction (proof "beyond a reasonable doubt") or even the lesser amount of proof (proof by a "preponderance of the evidence") that a plaintiff needs in order to win a civil case.

The requirement that searches be based on probable cause is not actually in the Fourth Amendment. It is an invention of the Supreme Court. What the Fourth Amendment actually does is, first, limit the use of warrants and, second, forbid searches and seizures, whether or not pursuant to warrant, if but only if they are unreasonable. Here is the text of the amendment: "The right of the people to be secure in their persons, houses, papers, and effects, against unreasonable searches and seizures, shall not be violated, and no Warrants shall issue, but upon probable cause, supported by Oath or affirmation, and particularly describing the place to be searched, and the persons or things to be seized." The only limitation on the search or seizure itself is reasonableness, a criterion flexible enough to allow the courts to calibrate the government's authority to make an arrest and conduct a search according to the gravity of the concern motivating those actions. Neither probable cause nor a warrant is a precondition found in the text of the amendment to a finding of reasonableness.

The curious structure of the amendment from a modern perspective—how it comes down harder on warrants than on warrantless searches and seizures—reflects the fact that its authors were particularly worried about searches pursuant to warrant because a warrant provided a legal defense to the officer conducting the search if he was sued for trespass. If general warrants, that is, warrants that did not satisfy the amendment's requirements of particularity and probable cause, could justify a search, the police would have carte blanche to search and seize. But in a typical upending of original understandings and disregard of pellucid constitutional text, the Supreme Court in the mid-twentieth century decided that the Fourth Amendment requires, where feasible, that a search be conducted pursuant to a warrant (though of course not a general warrant). This is not much of a filter, because a warrant proceeding is ex parte—the judge or magistrate hears only from the government. But the proceeding creates a written record that makes it easier for a court in which the legality of the search is subsequently challenged to determine whether it was reasonable. It has also spawned a complicated judge-made body of exceptions to the requirement of obtaining a warrant.

Exceptions there must be. Although often a warrant can be obtained within minutes by phone, this is not always possible; events may be moving too fast. If so—if, as the cases say, the circumstances are exigent—the requirement of getting a warrant is excused. And even though the Supreme Court has generally required that a warrantless arrest or search must, like an arrest or search based on a warrant, be supported by probable cause, "generally" is another important qualification. For remember that "probable cause" appears only in the warrant clause and that the legal criterion of a warrantless search is reasonableness. The Court has acknowledged the flexibility of the standard of reasonableness by holding that police can make a brief stop (called a "*Terry* stop" after the case that upheld its constitutionality) of a person, short of a full arrest, on the basis merely of a reasonable suspicion of criminal activity. During the stop they can question him in an effort to confirm or dispel their suspicions, and they can even pat him down to make sure he's not armed.

There are more stops of innocent people than there would be if probable cause were required, and that is a cost. But the cost per *Terry* stop is less than the cost of a full arrest because a brief stop causes less delay and embarrassment to the person stopped. That modest cost is offset by the benefit to law enforcement of allowing the police to make stops on suspicion, because in many cases the suspicion is confirmed and the police have solved one more crime.

Despite general approval of the *Terry* stop, the differential costs of different types or levels of search and seizure are a neglected consideration in discussions of the Fourth Amendment. The neglect is serious because the lower the cost to the person searched or seized, the less important it is to insist on strongly grounded suspicion. This consideration (a generalization from the *Terry* case) is especially important—and especially neglected—with respect to electronic eavesdropping. A physical search imposes costs in time, inconvenience, disruption, fear, and embarrassment on everyone searched; likewise an arrest, and even a *Terry* stop. But surreptitious eavesdropping need impose no costs at all on people who don't know they're being eavesdropped on, or who know but don't care because they have nothing they particularly care to hide from the eavesdropper. The latter is a more common situation than civil libertarians imagine. All manner of e-mail and other Internet "conversations" are monitored and recorded by employers and vendors. Probably most people would prefer to have their communications monitored by an agency interested only in national security than by their employer. And they would prefer either form of surveillance to a police search of their home, let alone to being arrested. It is easy to exaggerate the private as well as social harm from unobtrusive surveillance.

On the benefits side of a cost-benefit analysis (a type of analysis that a standard of "reasonableness" invites courts to conduct) of search and seizure, consider a case in which the police, having learned that a terrorist is driving to a city's downtown area in order to explode a car bomb, throw up roadblocks on all roads leading to the downtown and search every car. Since all the cars they stop except one are not carrying a bomb, they have no probable cause or even reasonable suspicion that a given car is the one they're looking for. Nevertheless, the Supreme Court suggested in *City of Indianapolis v. Edmond* and *Florida v. J.L.*, both decided in 2000, that such a dragnet would be reasonable and therefore lawful under the Fourth Amendment. The aggregate cost to innocent drivers in delay and inconvenience and the (limited) invasion of privacy would not be trivial. But it would be less than the expected cost of the car bombing. When the London transit system was bombed in July 2005, killing more than fifty people, the New York City police began random searches of subway riders' bags and parcels even though there was apparently no evidence that an attack was planned or imminent. The risk of an attack was slight, but so was the cost imposed by the very light searches.

In *Illinois v. Lidster* (2004), the Supreme Court, in an opinion by the liberal Justice Stephen Breyer, went even further, upholding a roadblock set up by the police to stop cars so that the drivers could be asked for information about a recent hit-and-run accident. Not only was there no individualized suspicion of the persons stopped; there was no collective suspicion. The purpose of the roadblock was not to stop the hit-and-run driver but to obtain information that might lead to his being apprehended elsewhere. Yet the Court held that the roadblock did not violate the Fourth Amendment. One factor the Court emphasized is that the stop was less intrusive than an arrest or a conventional search.

The *indiscriminate* character of a roadblock or other dragnet is, paradoxically, one of its redeeming features from a civil libertarian standpoint. Because no one is singled out, the opportunity for abuse by the authorities is reduced. This is an argument against profiling, which I take up in the next chapter.

LIDSTER IS IMPORTANT because it divorces searching from suspicion. It allows surveillance that invades liberty and privacy to be conducted because of the importance of the information sought, even if it is not sought for use in a potential criminal proceeding against the people actually under surveillance. National security intelligence is a quest for information in an analogous sense. Valuable intelligence might be extracted from conversations or other communications between innocent people—for example, one person telling a friend about a new neighbor who, unbeknownst to either party to the conversation, was a terrorist suspect—or at least people too loosely linked to terrorist activities to be prosecutable. Like the searchers in the *Lidster* case, intelligence officers have to cast their net very wide to obtain the information that they need in order to build up a picture of terrorist activities.

Congress overlooked this point when it enacted the Foreign Intelligence Surveillance Act (FISA) in 1978 and even when it amended the act in the USA PATRIOT Act shortly after the 9/11 attacks. The government had long engaged in wiretapping and other forms of electronic surveillance (and sometimes had conducted physical searches), including of U.S. citizens in the United States, aimed at obtaining information concerning possible foreign intrigues or other foreign threats against the nation. It had done these things without seeking warrants or trying to confine surveillance to situations in which there was probable cause to believe that the surveillance would uncover evidence of criminal activity. The Supreme Court in the *Keith* case (1972) had observed that what had become the conventional understanding (though, as we've seen, not always adhered to)—that a search or seizure must be based on probable cause to believe that a crime has occurred or is about to occur—might have to be relaxed when the goal of surveillance was to obtain intelligence information rather than evidence or leads for a criminal prosecution.

It was a prescient observation. The aim of national security intelligence is to thwart attacks by enemy nations or terrorist groups rather than just to punish the perpetrators after an attack has occurred. The threat of punishment is not a reliable deterrent to such attacks, especially when the attackers are fanatics who place a low value on their own lives and when the potential destructiveness of such attacks is so great that even a single failure of deterrence can have catastrophic consequences. That is why, when government is fighting terrorism rather than ordinary crime, the emphasis shifts from punishment to prevention. And prevention requires the intelligence agencies to cast a much wider and finer-meshed net in fishing for information. Once a crime has occurred, a focused search for the criminal and for evidence of the crime is feasible. But if the concern guiding a search is that a crime *might* occur, the focus has to be much broader. (I explain the difference between crime fighting and national security intelligence in chapter 4 of *Uncertain Shield*.)

The Foreign Intelligence Surveillance Act authorizes the issuance of warrants to conduct electronic surveillance aimed at obtaining "foreign intelligence information," defined as information relating to foreign threats to U.S. national security. (A warrant is not required in an emergency, but in that case the government must within seventy-two hours of the beginning of the surveillance seek retroactive authorization from the special court that issues FISA warrants.) A warrant may be issued only if there is probable cause to believe that the target of the surveillance is an "agent" of a foreign power or of a foreign group (such as a terrorist gang) or a "lone wolf"—an individual, not necessarily linked to any foreign nation or foreign group, who is engaged or preparing to engage in terrorist activities. If the target happens to be a "U.S. person" who is in the United States, a warrant cannot be issued unless there is probable cause to believe him actually involved in hostile activities against the United States. The category "U.S. person" consists primarily of U.S. citizens and permanent residents of the United States, thus excluding tourists, foreign students, illegal immigrants, and most other foreigners. With respect to those others, a warrant is required if at least one party to the communication is in the United States and the communication is intercepted in the United States.

Probable cause to believe that interception of the target's communications will yield evidence of crime need not be shown (though evidence of crime discovered in the course of a FISA search can be used to prosecute the perpetrators, provided that obtaining foreign intelligence information was a significant purpose of the interception). This departure from the ordinary requirements for getting a warrant is justified by the magnitude of the dangers that national security intelligence seeks to foil. The type of search the act authorizes is an a fortiori example of the category of searches recognized in cases such as *Lidster*. But since 9/11 the government has been making interceptions that FISA doesn't authorize, and we must consider whether such searches violate the Fourth Amendment.

According to the administration, these are just interceptions of communications to and from the United States in which one of the parties is suspected of terrorist connections, though the suspicion does not rise to the probable-cause level that would be required for obtaining a warrant. There may be more to the program, however. Most likely the next terrorist attack on the United States will, like the last one, be mounted from within the country but be orchestrated by leaders safely ensconced somewhere abroad. If a phone number in the United States is discovered to have been called by a known or suspected terrorist abroad, or if the number is found in the possession of a suspected terrorist or in a terrorist hideout, it would be prudent to intercept all calls, domestic as well as international, to or from that U.S. phone number and scrutinize them for suspicious content. But the mere fact that a suspected or even known terrorist has had a phone conversation with someone in the United States or has someone's U.S. phone number in his possession doesn't create probable cause to believe that the other person is also a terrorist; probably most phone conversations of terrorists are with people who are not themselves terrorists. The government can't get a FISA warrant just to find out whether someone *is* a terrorist; it has to already have a reason to believe he's one. Nor can it conduct surveillance of terrorist suspects who are not believed to have any foreign connections, because such surveillance would not yield *foreign* intelligence information.

FISA has yet another gap. A terrorist who wants to send a message can type it in his laptop and place it, unsent, in an e-mail account, which the intended recipient of the message can access by knowing the account name. The message itself is not communicated. Rather, it's as if the recipient had visited the sender and searched his laptop. The government, if it intercepted the e-mail from the intended recipient to the account of the "sender," could not get a FISA warrant to intercept (by e-mailing the same account) the "communication" consisting of the message residing in the sender's computer, because that message had never left the computer.

These examples suggest that surveillance outside the narrow bounds of FISA might significantly enhance national security. At a minimum, such surveillance might cause our foreign terrorist enemies to abandon or greatly curtail their use of telephone, e-mail, and other means of communicating electronically with people in the United States who may be members of terrorist sleeper cells. Civil libertarians believe that this is bound to be the effect of electronic surveillance, and argue that therefore such surveillance is futile. There is no "therefore." If the effect of electronic surveillance is to close down the enemy's electronic communications, that is a boon to us because it is far more difficult for terrorist leaders to orchestrate an attack on the United States by sending messages into the country by means of couriers. But what is far more likely is that some terrorists will continue communicating electronically, either through carelessness—the Madrid and London bombers were prolific users of electronic communications, and think of all the drug gangsters who are nailed by wiretaps—or in the mistaken belief that by using code words or electronic encryption they can thwart the NSA. (If they can, the program is a flop and will be abandoned.) There are careless people in every organization. If al-Qaeda is the exception, civil libertarians clearly are underestimating the terrorist menace! In all our previous wars, beginning with the Civil War, when telegraphic communications were intercepted, our enemies have known that we might intercept their communications, yet they have gone on communicating and we have gone on intercepting. As for surveillance of purely domestic communications, it would either isolate members of terrorist cells (which might, as I said, have no foreign links at all) from each other or yield potentially valuable information about the cells.

FISA's limitations are borrowed from law enforcement. When a crime is committed, the authorities usually have a lot of information right off the bat—time, place, victims, maybe suspects—and this permits a focused investigation that has a high probability of eventuating in an arrest. Not so with national security intelligence, where the investigator has no time, place, or victim and may have scant idea of the enemy's identity and location; hence the need for the wider, finer-meshed investigative net. It is no surprise that there have been leaks from inside the FBI expressing skepticism about the NSA program. This skepticism reflects the Bureau's emphasis on criminal investigations, which are narrowly focused and usually fruitful, whereas intelligence is a search for the needle in the haystack. FBI agents don't like being asked to chase down clues gleaned from the NSA's interceptions; 999 out of 1,000 turn out to lead nowhere. They don't realize that often the most that counterterrorist intelligence can hope to achieve is to impose costs on enemies of the nation (as by catching and "turning" some, or forcing them to use less efficient means of communication) in the hope of disrupting their plans. It is mistaken to think electronic surveillance a failure if it doesn't intercept a message giving the time and place of the next attack.

Whether surveillance outside FISA's limits is reasonable within the meaning of the Fourth Amendment depends not only on the likely efficacy of the surveillance but also on how seriously it invades privacy. Because of the volume involved, massive amounts of intercepted data must first be sifted by computers. The sifting can take two forms. One is a search for suspicious patterns or links; Mary DeRosa gives the example of searching for "use of a stolen credit card for a small purchase at a gas station—done to confirm whether the card is valid—before making a very significant purchase," a pattern suggestive of credit card fraud. The other form is the familiar Google-type search for more information about a known individual, group, subject, activity, identifier, and so on. A search for a social security number, for example, can reveal whether two similar or identical names are the names of two persons or one. The term "data mining" is sometimes limited to the first, the pattern search. But it is often used to embrace the second as well. I shall use the term in the broad sense.

The initial sifting is neither a search within the meaning of the Fourth Amendment nor "surveillance" within the meaning of FISA. Rather than invading privacy, computer sifting prevents most private data from being read by an intelligence officer or other human being by filtering them out. Depending on the search method used, data that are not selected for human scrutiny may not even be recorded and placed in a government database; they may merely be scanned by the computer while the data are being communicated ("packet sniffing").

The data that make the cut and are scrutinized by a human being will be those that contain clues to possible threats to national security, whether or not the clues are solid enough to base application for a FISA warrant on. The human scrutiny of private communications is a search, and most of the communications searched will turn out to be completely innocent. The principal worry about these searches from the standpoint of privacy, besides fear that hackers will gain access to the contents of the intercepted communications, is that those contents might be used to blackmail or otherwise intimidate the administration's critics and political opponents. A secondary fear is that they might be used to ridicule or embarrass. Such things have happened in the past, but they are less likely to happen today. Increased political partisanship, advances in communications technology, the growth of a culture of leaking and whistleblowing, and (related to the preceding point) more numerous and competitive media have converged to make American government a fishbowl. Secrets concerning matters that interest the public cannot be kept for long. The public would be even more avid to learn that public officials were using private information about American citizens for base political or personal ends than to learn that we have played rough with terrorist suspects—a matter that was quickly exposed despite efforts at concealment. Intense, unslaked public curiosity is a magnet to leakers and reporters.

Concerns with privacy could be alleviated, moreover, by adopting a rule forbidding the intelligence services to turn over any intercepted communications to the Justice Department for prosecution for any offense other than a violation of a criminal law intended for the protection of national security. Then people would not worry that unguarded statements in private conversations would get them into trouble. Such a rule would be a modification, urged in a parallel setting by Orin Kerr, of the "plain view" doctrine of search and seizure. That doctrine, another of the exceptions to the requirement of a warrant to search or seize, allows the seizure of evidence that the police discover in plain view in the course of an unrelated lawful search—even though the discovery is accidental and a warrant could not have been obtained to search for the evidence discovered.

But what if an intelligence officer, reading the transcript of a phone conversation that had been intercepted and then referred to him because the search engine had flagged it as a communication possibly possessing intelligence value, discovers that one of the parties to the communication seems to be planning a murder, though a murder having nothing to do with any terrorist plot? Must the officer ignore the discovery and refrain from notifying the authorities? Though the obvious answer is no, my answer is yes.

There is much wild talk in private conversations. Suppose the communication that has been intercepted and read for valid national security reasons contains the statement "I'll kill the son of a bitch." The probability will be very high that the statement is hyperbole, that there is no serious intent to kill anyone. But suppose intelligence officers have been told that if a communication they read contains evidence of crime, they should turn it over to the FBI. The officer in my hypothetical case does that, and the Bureau, since the matter has been referred to it by a government agency, takes the threat seriously and investigates (or turns the matter over to local police for investigation, if no federal crime is suspected). As word of such investigations got around, people would learn that careless talk in seemingly private conversations can buy them a visit from the FBI or the police. At this point the risk that national security surveillance would significantly deter candor in conversation would skyrocket. It is more important that the public tolerate extensive national security surveillance of communications than that an occasional run-of-the-mill crime go unpunished because intelligence officers were not permitted to share evidence of such a crime with law enforcement authorities. But if the evidence is of a crime related to national security, then sharing it with law enforcement authorities is appropriate and should be (and is) required. Other exceptions may be needed. Suppose that what is overheard is a conversation that identifies one of the parties as a serial killer. Serial killing is not terrorism, but it is such a serious crime that clues to it picked up in national security surveillance should be communicated to law enforcement authorities.

If such a rule (with its exceptions) were in place, I believe that the government could, in the present emergency, intercept *all* electronic communications inside or outside the United States, of citizens as well as of foreigners, without being deemed to violate the

Fourth Amendment, provided that computers were used to winnow the gathered data, blocking human inspection of intercepted communications that contained no clues to terrorist activity. We know that citizens (and permanent residents) can be terrorists operating against their country, even without any foreign links. The United States has had its share of U.S. citizen terrorists, such as the Unabomber and Timothy McVeigh and presumably whoever launched the anthrax attack on the East Coast in October 2001. The terrorist bombings of the London subway system in July 2005 were carried out by British citizens. And U.S. persons who are not terrorists or even terrorist sympathizers might have information of intelligence value—information they might be quite willing to share with the government if only they knew they had it. The information that enables an impending terrorist attack to be detected may be scattered in tiny bits that must be collected, combined, and sifted before their significance is apparent. Many of the bits may reside in the e-mails or phone conversations of innocent people, such as unwitting neighbors of terrorists, who may without knowing it have valuable counterterrorist information—one consequence of the jigsaw puzzle character of national security intelligence.

A further question, however, is whether the Fourth Amendment should be deemed to require warrants for such surveillance. The *Keith* case that I mentioned earlier held that warrants are required for conducting purely domestic surveillance even when the purpose is to protect national security, though the Court suggested that perhaps the probable-cause requirement could be attenuated. It would have to be. If the goal of surveillance is not to generate evidence of criminal activity but to detect terrorist threats, including those too incipient to be prosecutable as threats, and even threats of which the persons under surveillance may be unaware because the significance of the clues they possess eludes them, then to insist that the investigators establish probable cause to believe criminal activity is afoot will be to ask too much. The amendment's requirement of particularity of description of what is to be searched or seized would also have to be relaxed for surveillance warrants adequate to national security to be feasible, because intelligence officers will often not have a good idea of what they are looking for.

Given the Fourth Amendment's prohibition against general warrants and warrants not based on probable cause, it is questionable how much watering down of conventional warrant requirements the warrant clause of the Fourth Amendment would permit. Moreover, judicial review of a watered-down warrant application would not be an effective check on abuses. Warrants are intended for situations in which we do not want the police to do something (such as search one's home) without particularized grounds for believing that there is illegal activity going on. (That is true of physical searches, which FISA also authorizes, and there the warrant requirement should be retained.) All that the application for a warrant to conduct the kind of surveillance that I have described could say is that there is reason to believe that the surveillance might yield clues to terrorist identities, plans, or connections. What kind of filter could the court (the FISA court) asked to issue such warrants employ? Moreover, it is a secret court, composed of judges who are appointed by the chief justice of the United States without Senate confirmation, who are willing to undergo the background investigation required for a top-secret security clearance and so presumably are sympathetic to claims of national security, who hear only the government's side of the case because warrant proceedings are ex parte, and who are asked to issue a warrant to protect the nation against potential dangers far greater than that of ordinary crimes for which search warrants are sought. In such circumstances, the warrant would primarily—and perversely— serve its original function of shielding government officers from damages suits, since unless a warrant is procured fraudulently the officers who execute it will normally be shielded from civil liability.

We rightly worry when governmental power is concentrated, but a partial offset is that when power is concentrated so is responsibility. There would be fewer executions if the sentencing judge had to administer the lethal injection. It is better that the president assume the full responsibility for national security surveillance than that responsibility be diffused by enlisting the participation of judges under conditions in which they would be unable to exercise an effective check on executive power. We are not well served by judicial fig leaves.

But remember what I said in the Introduction—that calling a practice "constitutional" is not the bestowal of a compliment. Even if comprehensive warrantless electronic surveillance, domestic as well as foreign, would be constitutional in this age of global terrorism, it does not follow that there should be no statutory limitations. The executive branch contains many regulatory structures to channel and check the discretionary activities of civil servants, including national security personnel. The challenge is to design an appropriate structure for electronic surveillance that does not have the crippling limitations of FISA or fetishize judicial warrants.

Those crippling limitations, by the way, present their own constitutional problem. We are officially at war with al-Qaeda by virtue of the Authorization for Use of Military Force (see Chapter 3), and the collection of signals intelligence in wartime is a routine military tactic that Congress probably could not forbid without trenching on powers that Article II of the Constitution reserves to the president by making him commander in chief of the armed forces. The question thus is whether, despite the peculiar nature of the "war" with al-Qaeda, the NSA surveillance program should be regarded as being within the president's prerogative. If the answer is yes, then Congress's hands are tied; it is irrelevant that it may not have foreseen, when it issued the AUMF, that it was authorizing such surveillance. (Indeed, the AUMF itself may be irrelevant. No declaration of war is required to authorize the president to defend the United

States from attack, and if Osama bin Laden is to be believed, al-Qaeda remains in an attack posture vis-à-vis the United States.) If the answer is no, another question arises: whether the "law of necessity" could justify the president in violating FISA, the better to repel the terrorist threat to the nation.

The analysis ought not change if, throwing off the either-war-or-crime straitjacket, we ask simply whether the president's constitutional authority as commander in chief should be understood to allow him to conduct extensive electronic surveillance in the struggle against terrorism. Armed forces are used for many things besides waging conventional wars, and whatever they are used for, the president is the commander in chief, entitled to exercise the prerogatives of the position. As we know, the extent of those prerogatives is rendered unclear by Article I of the Constitution, which in granting Congress authority to "make Rules for the Regulation and Government" of the armed forces overlaps the president's authority as commander in chief. This does not matter if I am right that the Fourth Amendment does not bar surveillance more extensive than FISA appears to authorize.

CHAPTER FIVE

The Right of Free Speech, with a Comment on Profiling

IN MOTIVATION AND CHARACTER, terrorism is almost always political in a broad sense that includes religious aims, rather than being purely personal or commercial. Often it is a wing or extension of a political movement not itself violent, or is related to such a movement in some looser but still significant way. There are Muslim clergy who preach holy war and commend suicide bombing but do not themselves participate in or assist terrorist activities, although their inflammatory rhetoric may encourage such activities. They do not recruit terrorists but their rhetoric may make it easier for terrorists to recruit young men and women from among the imams' followers. Constitutional law as currently configured draws the line between incitement and advocacy. (Needless to say, it is not a distinction found in the constitutional text itself.) Incitement is a direct invitation to commit specific criminal acts in the immediate future and is punishable. Advocacy includes preaching the desirability of violent or otherwise criminal acts but without actually urging their commission forthwith, and is not punishable.

The preaching that I have described raises two issues of free-speech law. The first is whether it is proper for the government to use such preaching as a basis for investigation and surveillance. The second, an affirmative answer to which would require modification of the existing understanding of constitutionally protected speech, is whether it should be punishable. But there is a third free-speech issue, and it is the one with which I shall start. It arises not from the political character of terrorism but from the need to conceal information that either might aid the enemy directly, such as information about the design of weapons of mass destruction, or might weaken our response to terrorism by publicizing the distasteful methods that may be indispensable elements of that response.

To take the second of these concerns first, the pros and cons of coercive interrogation, of "rendition" (sending a prisoner to a nation that may use torture), even of torture—and more generally of "covert action" as practiced abroad by the CIA—are more evenly balanced than civil libertarians are willing to acknowledge, as we have seen. But the cons are almost certain to predominate in the international court of public opinion if the methods themselves, or the operations that utilize them, are publicized. Secrecy is essential. And it cannot be secured merely by having laws that forbid the disclosure of classified information. It is too easy for possessors of such information to leak it without running a significant risk of detection. To keep it secret the government must be able to punish the media when they knowingly publish it. It would be quite natural to deem the media accomplices of the leaker, akin to receivers of stolen property, when they publish material that they know is classified. But the Supreme Court held in *New York Times Co. v. United States* (1971) that the *Times* could not be enjoined from publishing the Pentagon Papers even though it knew they were classified. The Court said that to enjoin publication would be to impose a "prior restraint" on speech, equivalent to requiring that a prospective publication be submitted to a censorship board.

Censorship was, as I noted in Chapter 1, the particular concern of the framers of the free-speech clause of the First Amendment. Indeed, to them freedom of speech and freedom from censorship were virtual synonyms. But the clause has never been interpreted to forbid *all* censorship. A CIA officer who wants to publish a book about his experiences must submit the manuscript to the agency for approval in advance of publication, even if he has left the agency's employ. That is censorship, and the Supreme Court has held that it is constitutional. There was no justification for the different approach taken in the Pentagon Papers case. True, CIA officers sign a contract in which they agree to submit their manuscripts to the agency for approval; but to receive a security clearance, *any* individual, whether or not employed by the government, must sign a nondisclosure agreement, which means agreeing to subject himself to censorship.

The government should not be allowed to shield itself from public criticism by classifying whatever materials it wants. Government agencies frequently classify material not because it contains secrets that would endanger the nation if revealed to the public but because publication would embarrass the agency by revealing its mistakes or would provide helpful information to a rival agency. Overclassification creates a culture of secrecy that inhibits the production and flow of information to which the public should be entitled. The *Times* should have been permitted to challenge the classification of the Pentagon Papers as a violation of the First Amendment but should not have been given carte blanche to publish national security secrets. The Supreme Court held in the *Carpenter* case in 1987 that it is a federal crime to sell stock on the basis of confidential information revealed by a publisher's disloyal employee. Why doubt that the Constitution authorizes Congress to criminalize the sale of newspapers on the basis of military secrets, or other equally sensitive confidential information, revealed by a disloyal federal employee?

A curiosity of the Pentagon Papers case is that several of the justices left open the possibility that the *Times* and its editors could have been prosecuted criminally as accomplices to Daniel Ellsberg, who was prosecuted under the Espionage Act of 1917 for leaking the Pentagon Papers to the *Times* and the *Washington Post*. In a later case, *Bartnicki v. Vopper* (2001), the Court said that "it would be quite remarkable to hold that speech by a law-abiding possessor of information can be suppressed in order to deter conduct by a non-law-abiding third party." But this misses the point that an accomplice is not "law-abiding."

The Espionage Act is one of several federal statutes that punish leakers, but unlike the United Kingdom's Official Secrets Act, our statutes do not constitute a seamless prohibition of leaks of even properly classified material, and have rarely resulted in successful prosecutions. The prosecution of Ellsberg collapsed because of government misconduct in prosecuting him, but he might anyway have been acquitted on substantive grounds. Subsection (d) of the Espionage Act, under which he was charged, requires that the leaker have had "reason to believe [that the information he leaked] could be used to the injury of the United States or to the advantage of any foreign nation." A jury might have doubted that revealing the contents of the Pentagon Papers had hurt the United States or helped any foreign country, even North Vietnam.

Other statutes punish the leaking of classified information relating to technical means of intelligence, such as electronic surveillance, or communicating classified information to a foreign government. But no statute explicitly punishes journalists or media for publishing illegally leaked classified material. The absence of an Official Secrets Act is one reason our government is such a sieve. The absence reflects a national culture of nosiness, and of distrust of government bordering on paranoia.

However, since the Espionage Act does punish the communication of material relating to national defense (surely including defense against modern terrorism) that could be used to injure the nation, it is difficult to see why the publication of such material, which obviously is a form of communication and would seem, therefore, to violate the act, should not be enjoinable in advance. A principal purpose of criminal punishment is to deter crime by confronting would-be criminals with the threat of punishment. Authorizing criminal punishment thus reflects a social judgment that the activity criminalized should not take place. If it should not take place, why should it not be enjoined?

The usual answer is that because more proof is required for a criminal conviction than for an injunction, disallowing the latter is protective of speech. The answer is unsatisfactory. Not only can a criminal penalty be made severe enough to have the same effect, via deterrence, as an injunction, and not only, as Frederick Schauer has argued, might a risk-averse publisher prefer to be told in advance that he cannot publish something rather than risk publishing it and being thrown in prison for his trouble. In addition, the cost to national security of speech that reveals classified material could well exceed the benefit of such speech, and in that event an injunction, if that is the more effective remedy, would increase rather than reduce social welfare.

It should come as no surprise that despite the Pentagon Papers decision, the government *can* enjoin the publication of highly sensitive classified material. (I give an example later.) It can certainly censor military secrets in wartime, and we are at war, or at least quasi-war, with a terrorist network that is more dangerous than some of the nations that we have warred against. So in the end, as is usual in American law, the scope of a constitutional right that touches on national security is determined by balancing liberty interests—the interest in being allowed to publish anything one wants to publish and to read anything that anyone can find a publisher willing to publish, along with a broader communal interest in the free exchange of ideas, information, and opinions—against the public safety. But by embracing the "prior restraints" taboo, the Supreme Court placed a thumb on the balance, arbitrarily increasing the weight of free speech. (Maybe the Court just *thought* it was doing this, however, given the possibility of severe punishment ex post.) As a matter of constitutional law, the government should be allowed to prevent or punish the knowing publication or other dissemination of classified material concerning national security, provided that the material was classified in accordance with proper statutory criteria (which do not yet exist).

The qualification in the last sentence is vital. A genuine First Amendment issue is presented by efforts of government to bottle up information to which the public is entitled because publicity would not endanger national security. (That "bottling" was described in a well-known book by Daniel Patrick Moynihan.) Courts asked to enjoin publication of classified material should demand a concrete explanation *in camera* for why concealing the material from the public is reasonably required for the protection of national security.

Even with this qualification, there is a double-edged quality to punishing the publication of classified materials. By reducing the number of leaks, such punishment reduces the amount of whistleblowing. Our government's porous structure, made more so by the absence of a U.S. Official Secrets Act, undermines national security and personal privacy, but it also reduces the likelihood of abuse inherent in the government's wielding broad powers to protect national security.

The other censorship issue that the current emergency presents involves the freedom to publish the fruits of scientific research, in particular biological research. An acute danger in the modern age is the potential use of bioengineering techniques by terrorists to increase the lethality of pathogens, such as the smallpox virus. Several years ago a team of Australian biologists developed a lethal virus by injecting mouse DNA into mousepox virus. Mousepox is closely related to smallpox but is far less lethal. The enhanced mousepox virus, however, was so potent that it killed even mice that had been vaccinated against mousepox. The scientists (whose work was later successfully replicated by scientists at St. Louis University in the United States) published an article in a leading scientific journal describing the enhanced mousepox virus and in a part of the article captioned "materials and methods" provided a blueprint for any bioterrorist able to obtain a virus that causes disease in human beings and could be enhanced by the method employed by the Australian scientists.

Efforts to censor publication of biological research would probably be futile because there are thousands of biological journals, most published outside the United States. But it is an interesting analytical question whether such censorship would violate the First Amendment. No categorical answer can be given. The important point is that the press, whether popular or scholarly, should not enjoy a blanket immunity from measures sensibly designed to protect national security by the least restrictive means possible.

DOMESTIC INTELLIGENCE, currently the responsibility mainly of the Federal Bureau of Investigation, seeks to foil attacks on the nation from within. The 9/11 attacks, which originated at U.S. airports and were conducted by individuals who had resided in the United States for months or even (intermittently) for years, are an example. Any conscientious domestic intelligence officer would want to maintain a close watch on radical imams in the U.S. Muslim community of several million people (the exact number is unknown, but three million is the most common estimate) even if there is no basis for thinking that any of these imams has yet crossed the line that separates advocacy from incitement. In fact, some have been convicted of terrorism-related crimes and others may have acquaintances among the active supporters and practitioners of Islamist terrorism. Fiery preachings may impel votaries to join terrorist cells or provide financial aid or other assistance to terrorists. The FBI may therefore want to send intelligence officers into the mosques at which radical imams preach, masquerading as members of the congregation. It may want to bribe actual members to spy for it and to report what the imams say and how the congregation responds. It may want to collect from public sources as much information as it can about the imams and the enthusiasts in their congregations, or even follow the imams and the enthusiasts around and photograph or eavesdrop on them. For all one knows, the Bureau is doing these things today.

Insofar as it is merely collecting information by the means just described, it is not, under existing understandings of the First Amendment, infringing anyone's freedom of speech. But are those understandings correct? Knowledge that FBI agents were circulating throughout the congregation—surreptitiously taking notes and maybe photographing or recording the proceedings, recruiting members of the congregation to spy on other members and on the imam, collecting information about him and his followers and maybe putting a "tail" on him or on them—would have a dampening effect on the free expression of beliefs. Maybe the imam himself (by assumption a radical, and probably deeply committed to the cause) would not be deterred. But some of his followers, especially the most recent and least fully committed ones, would be. Other members of the Muslim community would be discouraged from joining the congregation in the first place. Freedom of speech would, as a practical matter, be curtailed. But it does not follow that it would be infringed. That is a legal conclusion, the validity of which would hinge on the importance of the investigative activities to national security. If they are important, a modest limitation of speech resulting from induced self-censorship, which probably is all that the activities would cause, may be a price worth paying.

A further reason to doubt the impact of such a limitation on the marketplace of ideas and opinion is the low social value of radical Islamist rhetoric. Although civil libertarians blanch at the thought of attempting to assess the value of particular views advanced by political advocates—"viewpoint discrimination" is about the worst offense against freedom of speech that civil libertarians can imagine—that is too squeamish a reaction. In the context of American society, the advocacy of a holy war against the United States, the West generally, our allies in Asia and Africa, Western values, and modernity in general has no redeeming social value; it is merely crazy and murderous. Of course you could not prove this to the radical imams, as you might be able to prove a scientific proposition to them. The truths of science are universal, those of morality and politics local. But local culture sets limits to fruitful debate by ruling certain viewpoints off the agenda; to deny this is relativism run wild.

Granted, there is danger in setting those limits prematurely. But it is a greater danger when the issue (discussed below) is whether to outlaw a particular viewpoint rather than just ascribe a low value to it for purposes of determining whether its advocates can be investigated. Preaching the destruction of the West in the name of Islam is sufficiently outlandish to allay concern that if the FBI places radical imams under surveillance, ideas of value to America will not receive as full-throated an expression as they would if such surveillance were forbidden. The wildest, most irresponsible, most hateful speech may contain nuggets of insight, but not enough to place the control of such speech beyond the reach of government if there is convincing evidence that the speech is likely to lead, sooner or later, to acts of terrorism. In this respect Islamic extremism is different from communism. The communist movement was odious and threatening, but communist ideas were, perhaps still are, within the mainstream of Western thought. The same cannot be said of preaching holy war against the West.

There are additional costs to the monitoring of such preaching, however, because extremist speech is not the only thing that will be going on in the mosque—the imam himself may alternate hateful sermons with innocuous ones—and the surveillance may drive away members of the congregation whose participation in the activities of the mosque is limited to lawful speech and religious activities. Nevertheless, the benefits to national security of keeping tabs on advocates of Islamist violence, even if the advocates are not themselves violent—even if they merely preach bitter hatred of the West—are likely to outweigh the costs in diminished freedom of speech. The government appears to have had little success in penetrating terrorist cells, here or abroad (we cannot even be certain that there are terrorist cells in the United States, although we cannot afford to assume that there are not). Success will probably require working inward toward the cells from the outer fringes of terrorist activity—the financial supporters, the new recruits, the groupies and hangers-on, the relatives, the silent sympathizers, the followers of the radical imams, and the imams themselves. The terrorist danger is great enough to justify efforts to work inward toward, and eventually into, the cells by means of the investigative methods that I have sketched. At least it is great enough to rebut a charge that these methods are unconstitutional, though prudence may induce the FBI to stop considerably short of the investigative limits that the Constitution (as I would interpret it) fixes, in order to maintain good relations with the U.S. Muslim community.

Sensitivity to the possible effect of national security investigations on freedom of political expression lay behind the Levi guidelines, promulgated by the Department of Justice, headed at the time by Edward H. Levi, in 1976. The guidelines authorized a "full investigation" of a political group by the FBI only when there was reason to believe that the group "may be engaged in activities which involve the use of force or violence and which involve or will involve the violation of federal law." The problem with this formulation is that while a group may not *yet* be engaged in any such activity, it may be planning to engage in it or thinking of engaging in it and may have overlapping membership, finances, and so on with groups engaged in or planning such activity. In explaining why the "may be engaged" standard was too restrictive, my court ruled in the 1984 *Alliance to End Repression v. City of Chicago* case, when the terrorist threat was much weaker than it is now, that the government must be permitted to

> investigate any group that advocates the commission, even if not immediately, of terrorist acts in violation of federal law. It need not wait till the bombs begin to go off, or even till the bomb factory is found. We are not speaking metaphorically. Between 1970 and 1980, domestic terrorist organizations committed more than 400 bombings in the United States. The FBI cannot hope to nip terrorist conspiracies in the bud if it may not investigate proto-terrorist organizations. That is why . . . the FBI would not be violating the First Amendment . . . if it decided to investigate a threat that was not so immediate as to permit punitive measures against the utterer. Since the repressive effect of an investigation is less than that of a prosecution but the benefits in preventing violent crime may be as great, a less immediate danger will justify the government's action. Admittedly the repressive effect will not be zero. No one wants his name in an FBI investigatory file; and the knowledge that the FBI investigates groups that advocate violent change could deter some people from joining such groups and deter the groups themselves from engaging in lawful though minatory forms of advocacy. There would therefore be a cost to the values protected by the First Amendment, if the groups never stepped over the boundary that

separates privileged from indictable speech. But we think the cost would be outweighed by the benefits in preventing crimes of violence, provided that the FBI did not prolong its investigation after it became clear that the only menace of a group under investigation was rhetorical and ideological.

The organizations in which the Bureau was interested were not religious, and there is a natural sensitivity about investigating religious organizations on the basis of sermons. But the sensitivity is misplaced when religion and violence merge. The merger is not unknown to Christianity; priests played an active role in Catholic plots to kill Queen Elizabeth I and replace her with Mary, Queen of Scots. But Jesus Christ was the opposite of a warrior priest; Muhammad, in contrast, was a general. Terrorism and religion are tightly entwined in Muslim extremism today; the juncture cannot be ignored by our security services.

A BROADER PROGRAM of surveillance, aimed not at radical imams or other extremists as such but at the Muslim community in the United States, a community overwhelmingly composed of loyal U.S. citizens, might be challenged as a denial not of free speech but of the equal protection of the laws. Let me interrupt my consideration of free-speech issues to consider that possibility.

Although the equal protection clause of the Fourteenth Amendment is applicable only to state action, not to action by the federal government, the Supreme Court has held that racial and other forms of discrimination that would be unconstitutional if engaged in by states violate the Fifth Amendment's due process clause if engaged in by the federal government. In the *Korematsu* case (1944), which upheld the military order, issued shortly after the Pearl Harbor attack, banishing Japanese Americans from the West Coast, the Supreme Court assumed that were it not for military necessity, such a racially or ethnically discriminatory measure would violate the due process clause. Yet the case was decided years before the Court held that equal protection of the laws is a component of due process of law and therefore a constraint on the federal government as well as on the states.

The general issue is the constitutionality of profiling based on race, ethnicity, or some other ground regarded as invidious. At one level, such profiling is unexceptionable. If witnesses report a theft by a young black male, it would be absurd for the police to look for suspects among other groups in the population. Profiling becomes problematic only when the differential probability of guilt is much smaller. But one must distinguish between ordinary crimes and Islamist terrorism, and in the latter category between profiling U.S. citizens and profiling foreigners.

Consider a policy of disproportionately frequent searches of vehicles driven by Hispanics because Hispanics are disproportionately involved in illegal drug trafficking. The policy would have some effect on the crime rate, but probably not a great effect. Driving one class of suppliers out of business makes room for others. Given a fixed budget for law enforcement, the increased apprehension of Hispanic drug couriers would be offset by a reduced risk to non-Hispanics of being apprehended for transporting drugs, and so non-Hispanics would flock to replace the Hispanics as couriers. The ethnic composition of the illegal workforce would be altered by profiling, but the crime rate would be affected only to the extent that Hispanics were more efficient drug couriers because of language and other ties to major countries that produce drugs.

In the case of terrorism, a similar replacement effect can be anticipated. Assume a fixed budget for screening airline passengers and a reallocation of funds within the budget limit to enable more young male airline passengers of Middle Eastern origin to be subjected to intensive screening, as distinguished from the limited screening to which all passengers are subjected. Then fewer passengers who did not fit the profile would be screened, and this would induce terrorist groups to make greater use of women and of men who either were not of Middle Eastern origin or did not appear to be. The supply of such substitute terrorists may not be as great as that of non-Hispanic drug couriers, but it is not trivial and its existence would reduce the effect of profiling. A growing number of Islamist terrorists are European converts to Islam, and it would certainly make sense for the terrorist leaders to be focusing on recruiting among those converts in order to circumvent ethnic profiling. This is the same analysis that advises against concentrating too many of our counterterrorist resources on the protection of New York and Washington, since terrorists can substitute other targets.

The benefits of profiling airline passengers are thus likely to be modest—even negative if profiling causes us to lower our guard against terrorist converts. And the costs may be great in the case of Muslims who are U.S. citizens or lawful permanent residents. Being singled out on the basis of ethnicity is intensely resented and could undermine the loyalty to the United States of people who have ethnic and religious ties to the nation's enemies, as American Muslims do. The argument for profiling is further undermined if we relax the assumption of a fixed security budget. By increasing the budget for airline security it becomes possible to screen everybody more carefully.

An intermediate solution might be to subject more U.S. citizens who are Muslim or of apparent Middle Eastern origin to intensive screening than other citizens, but also to subject enough of the other citizens to such screening that the profiled group did not feel blatantly discriminated against. To subject all citizens to the same very high level of screening, however, might be prohibitively costly.

The situation with regard to noncitizens is different. They are not expected to be loyal to the United States, and so the concern with alienating them by subjecting them to profiling is less acute. The concern is further attenuated by the fact that no foreigner expects to be treated identically to a citizen. However, for this purpose a lawful permanent resident should probably be equated to a citizen rather than to a foreigner, since permanent residence is normally a stepping-stone to citizenship.

Although profiling on the basis of ethnicity is undoubtedly discriminatory, and discrimination on such a basis is usually deemed unconstitutional, there is no better reason for an absolute rule against this discrimination than for an absolute rule against restrictions on freedom of speech. Affirmative action is a form of racial discrimination, but the Supreme Court permits it. The prohibition against restricting free speech is, as we are about to see, riddled with exceptions.

As usual, there is need to strike a balance. On one hand, the contribution of ethnic profiling to security against terrorism is probably positive but only modestly so: it's just a cost saver; the enemy may be able to circumvent it (though not costlessly) by altering his recruitment policy; and it risks alienating a community we very much want on our side. On the other hand, the discrimination involved in being searched more often at airports than other passengers are searched is mild relative to such historical measures of racial or ethnic discrimination as the banishment of Japanese Americans from the West Coast at the beginning of World War II, the segregation of the races in the public schools of the South, or discrimination in employment or in admission to elite schools. The balance is close enough to warrant leaving the matter to be governed by policy rather than prohibited as a matter of constitutional law.

The form of "profiling" that consists of keeping a careful watch on preachers of holy war is least subject to the objections to profiling. It would be preposterous to tell the FBI that if it wants to conduct surveillance of mosques it must conduct the same level of surveillance of churches and synagogues. There is no danger of a replacement effect as a result of differential surveillance: al-Qaeda will not be able to recruit non-Muslim clergy to preach holy war.

A MORE DIFFICULT CONSTITUTIONAL QUESTION than whether advocacy of terrorism (short of incitement) can be investigated is whether it can be outlawed. Much of that advocacy consists of efforts to stir up hatred against Americans, Jews, and the West. The general assumption is that "hate speech" is protected by the First Amendment unless it has a very specific target, as when the Ku Klux Klan burns a cross in front of a black family's home (*Virginia v. Black* [2003]). Cross-burning is "speech" in the sense of expression of opinion—wordless symbolic communication is often more expressive than literal speech. But, depending on context, it can also be a threat. And threats are among the many exceptions to the constitutional right of free speech. If, however, a radical imam merely preaches the glory of suicide bombing without naming a specific target, the "threat" is too diffuse to be punishable under the current understanding of the constitutional scope of free speech.

Hate speech is really not a good analogy to the extremist rhetoric found in radical Islamic preaching. The focus of efforts to ban hate speech, notably on college campuses but also in the cross-burning case, is on the fear or emotional distress that the speech causes to the target. That is a significant harm, but less serious than the potential harm from speech that induces terrorist activity. So the fact that the First Amendment has been interpreted to forbid punishing hate speech, with the narrow exception illustrated by the cross-burning case, should not determine whether speech that encourages terrorism is punishable.

As usual, the constitutional text does not resolve the issue. It does not define "freedom of speech," and from the beginning the term has been understood to exclude a variety of forms of expression; among them are libel and slander, copyright infringement, product disparagement, criminal solicitations, disclosure of military secrets, publication of purloined trade secrets, political assassinations (an especially vivid form of political expression), obscenity, certain invasions of privacy, some anonymous political campaign literature, false advertising, nude dancing, indecent language on radio and television, and perjury, as well as incitements and other threats.

The incitement/threat category could be expanded, without doing violence to either the constitutional text or the methodology of balancing that has determined the actual scope of freedom of speech, to include generalized advocacy of violence against the United States. That was in fact the law of free speech as late as 1951, when the Supreme Court in the *Dennis* case upheld the constitutionality of the Smith Act. The act, which was aimed at the Communist Party though the party itself was not outlawed, made it a crime to advocate the forcible overthrow of the government of the United States.

But in 1969, in the *Brandenburg* case, the Court backtracked and held that speech advocating violence or other criminal conduct cannot constitutionally be suppressed unless it is "directed to inciting or producing imminent lawless action and is likely to incite or produce such action." Requiring proof that the speaker intended to produce imminent lawless conduct and was likely to achieve his goal is an insurmountable obstacle to punishing advocates of holy war. Preachings by radical imams that merely create an atmosphere conducive to recruiting terrorists, like communist agitation that merely facilitated Soviet recruitment of spies and penetration of labor unions, government agencies, and other institutions, lack the imminence of threat required for punishment under the *Brandenburg* standard.

To make imminence a sine qua non of limiting freedom of speech is simply another way of placing a thumb on the constitutional balance. Imminence is certainly a relevant factor, even without discounting future harms to present value. The more remote a harm is, the less likely it is actually to materialize and (what is really just an aspect of the same point) the greater the government's opportunity to take other steps, besides suppressing the speech, to prevent the harm from materializing. But imminence is not the only relevant factor. A huge harm unlikely to materialize for several more years is not a lesser threat to the nation than a much smaller harm likely to materialize tomorrow. To tell Congress and the president that they can do nothing to prevent forms of advocacy likely to multiply the number of future terrorists makes no more sense than telling them that they cannot prevent the publication of recipes for bioweapons because it would probably take years to get from the recipe to the actual manufacture, let alone use, of the weapons.

There is irony in civil libertarians' defense of a requirement of imminence. They are less concerned with the current impact—surely slight—on civil liberties of the USA PATRIOT Act, the National Security Agency's "secret" program of electronic surveillance, and other security measures adopted by the Bush administration than with where such measures might lead. Why should those future prospects be given greater weight than the possible future consequences of radical Islamist agitation?

Civil libertarians will reply that as long as the harmful consequences lie in the future, there is an antidote in the form of counterspeech. That is fine if the agitator is merely appealing to abstract, debatable principles. But if he is issuing instructions (how to create an explosive belt for use in suicide bombing, for example) or appealing to the exploitive or malicious feelings of his audience, it is unclear what counterarguments are available to opponents.

Brandenburg is an illustration of the Supreme Court's proclivity for laying down rules. The judiciary is a bureaucracy, and bureaucracies are kept in line by rules. Like the head of any bureaucracy, the Court cannot monitor and if necessary correct every decision by its underlings, the judges of the state and lower federal courts. It can control them only by rules. But rules usually don't make sense without exceptions. The *Brandenburg* rule is a good example. A rule that in the name of freedom of speech forbids punishing preachers of holy war against the West while allowing the punishing of the false advertising of a weight-loss pill is excessively lacking in nuance.

All this is not to suggest that the Supreme Court should uncritically accept the government's claims concerning the dangerous consequences of extremist rhetoric. The government has a conflict of interest, because its paramount duty is to protect national security. If it could be trusted to hold national security and civil liberties concerns in perfect equipoise, there would be no need for judicial checks. But arbitrary rules do not adequately discharge the Court's duty to hold the balance even between the interest in national security and the interest in personal liberty. If the government leans too far on one side, the ACLU, itself an interest group, leans too far on the other.

In any event, few serious students of the First Amendment think that the "rule" of the *Brandenburg* case is to be taken literally, though the Court has not yet said anything to cast doubt on its continued validity. Civil libertarians do not much criticize *United States v. Progressive, Inc.* (1979), which enjoined a magazine from publishing classified material about the hydrogen bomb, even though the decision flunks the imminence test. It is a disservice to judges to treat their general statements, which necessarily reach beyond the facts of the particular cases in which they are made, as if they were statutes. Clarence Brandenburg was not Osama bin Laden; he was merely a Grand Dragon of the Ohio Ku Klux Klan. The Ku Klux Klan, a shadow of its old self by the 1960s, was not the Comintern. The *Dennis* and *Brandenburg* tests should be understood as domain-specific.

But the fact that *Brandenburg* is not the last word on the government's authority to rein in extremist rhetoric that falls short of incitement doesn't mean that we should enact laws forbidding generalized advocacy of violence against the United States. Apart from obvious definitional problems, there are two objections. One is that no need for such laws in this country, as distinct from countries that have restive Muslim populations, has been shown. At least no immediate need; there have been only a few cases reported so far of radical imams in the United States urging support of terrorism or going into prisons to try to convert prisoners to Islamist extremism. In the present circumstances the enactment of laws forbidding radical Islamist expression would be needlessly provocative. The situation may change—and with it, one hopes, the *Brandenburg* test. Even in radical Islamist communities, the percentage of people willing to commit terrorist acts or even assist terrorists in meaningful ways is small. But when one reflects that there are several million Muslims in the United States and that a tiny number of terrorists may be able to cause catastrophic harm to a nation, the government should not have to stand by helplessly while radical imams convert a multitude to their radical creed.

Ironically, a stronger argument can be made today for punishing hate speech directed against Muslims than for punishing extremist rhetoric by Muslims. Recall the furor created by the publication in Denmark of cartoons making fun of Muhammad. The cartoons could hardly be thought a significant contribution to the marketplace of ideas and opinions, and they may have stirred greater hatred of the West than any sermon by an extremist imam has done. A single foreign incident of that kind hardly justifies revising our constitutional understandings to place hate speech in the same category as incitement. But we should be thinking ahead to a time when hateful attacks in the United States on Islam may present a clear threat to retaining the loyalty of the U.S. Muslim community; we should keep doctrine flexible against such a day.

Another objection to punishing extremist advocacy is that by driving radical expression underground it would deprive intelligence and law-enforcement agencies of a valuable source of information about potential threats to national security. Legal activities can be monitored more easily than illegal ones, because the former are conducted above ground, ordinarily with little or no attempt at concealment.

This suggests, by the way, that investigating extremist advocacy by means that do not trigger constitutional challenge may actually be a more effective method of combating terrorism than punishing such advocacy. Recall from Chapter 4 that the aim of the National Security Agency's program of warrantless surveillance is to discover terrorist identities and plans rather than to facilitate the prosecution of known terrorists. Discovery usually enables prevention without need to invoke the criminal process, an invocation that the intelligence community tends to resist because of the attendant publicity; it doesn't want terrorist groups to realize they've been penetrated.

But this is not a book about how best to respond to the terrorist threat. It is a book about the limitations that constitutional law places on the government's responses to the threat. The Bill of Rights should not be interpreted so broadly that any measure that does not strike the judiciary as a sound response to terrorism is deemed unconstitutional. That would place the judges in charge of national security. That laws forbidding extremist speech would be, in my judgment, unsound at the present time is no reason to think that they would be unconstitutional.

CHAPTER SIX

Rights of Privacy

THE AMERICAN PUBLIC worries more about invasions of privacy than about summary proceedings against suspected terrorists, curtailments of the freedom of speech of the law-abiding, or the right of the media to publish government secrets. Few Americans fear being accused of links to terrorism, fewer still wish to speak out in support of terrorists, and most recognize the legitimacy of keeping the operational details of programs for fighting terrorism secret. But almost everyone places a high value on his privacy. Yet the "right of privacy," which has become such a cockpit of constitutional debate though nowhere mentioned in the Constitution, does not refer to privacy in the usual senses of enjoying some peace and quiet (seclusion) and of being able to conceal personal information about oneself (secrecy). It refers instead to sexual and reproductive freedom. So Americans now have constitutional rights, created by the Supreme Court without any basis in the constitutional text, to use contraceptives, to have an abortion, and to engage in homosexual sex. But there are only hints that they might have a constitutional right to seclusion or secrecy.

Some constitutional provisions, either literally or as interpreted by the Supreme Court, do protect—but only, as it were, by accident—one or the other of these interests, and sometimes both. The prohibition against requiring religious oaths for public office; the interpretation of the First Amendment as permitting (in most situations) anonymous publication; the Third Amendment's prohibition against quartering troops in private homes in peacetime; the Fourth Amendment's prohibition against unreasonable searches and seizures of one's person, houses, papers, or effects (a prohibition that includes the Postal Service's reading the letters it carries and that has, as we know, been extended to wiretapping and other means of electronic interception); and the Fifth Amendment's prohibition against compelled self-incrimination all have the effect of guaranteeing a measure of privacy in the two normal senses of the word, senses unrelated to the modern constitutional right of (sexual and reproductive) privacy. That is, they create rights to be left alone by the government in one's private space (seclusion) and to conceal a variety of beliefs, assertions, personal information, and behaviors from the government (secrecy).

Although seclusion and secrecy (but not sexual and reproductive freedom) were well-understood aspects of privacy in the eighteenth century, the concern of the Constitution's framers, in the various provisions that I have mentioned, was with protecting property rights and political rights rather than with protecting seclusion and secrecy for their own sake. They are, it is true, among the motivations for wanting to keep the police from entering one's home, rummaging through one's things, and reading one's private papers. But the scope and the purpose of a legal protection need not coincide. The fact that the Fourth Amendment gives some protection to the secrecy interest needn't imply that anything that invades that interest violates the amendment. The much-criticized *Olmstead* decision, which held that wiretapping that does not involve a trespass (the tap is usually attached to the telephone line outside the premises of the person whose phone conversations are being intercepted) is not a search or seizure within the meaning of the Fourth Amendment, not only had a sound historical pedigree and conformed to the language of the amendment, which refers to the search or seizure only of solid objects (persons, houses, papers, and effects), but also reflected the difference between searches that invade the seclusion interest in privacy—and usually the secrecy interest as well (the search is for something that the target of the search had tried to conceal)—and searches that invade only the latter interest. Compare entering a person's house and stealing his computer to obtain the files with removing the files by hacking into the computer via the Internet. That is not to say that *Olmstead* was decided correctly. Language and drafters' intent are not the only or even, in my judgment, the best guides to constitutional rule making; they are merely the most orthodox ones.

The idea that there should be a general right of privacy, including privacy of communications, emerged long after the Constitution was drafted. First urged by Samuel Warren and Louis Brandeis in a law review article in 1890 (though without reference to communications), it gradually became a part of the common law of most states, although it was not yet a well-established right when *Olmstead* was decided. In constitutional cases, other than ones involving wiretapping and other electronic eavesdropping, it figures more often as a constitutional value than as a constitutional right—that is, as a social interest, like the interest in public safety, that limits the scope of constitutional rights. The Court has upheld against First Amendment challenges laws limiting the volume of sound trucks used to broadcast political messages; the noise from the sound trucks invades the peace and quiet—the seclusion—of people within the range of the sound. The Court has allowed city governments to place limits on the routes taken by political marchers, in order to minimize interference with the routines of other people in the city. But it has invalidated laws that prohibit the media from publishing the names of rape victims.

When freedom of speech and privacy as seclusion or secrecy collide, freedom of speech usually wins out.

The privacy interest that is particularly relevant to the present national emergency is the interest in concealing personal information about oneself, although a quarantine or other aggressive public health measure imposed in an effort to limit the effects of a biological attack would invade people's personal space, as do physical searches.

Since national security intelligence is concerned with learning the identity of terrorists and their supporters rather than just learning more about known terrorists, some of the personal information gathered by intelligence agencies pertains to people who have no links to terrorism; they are fish too small to eat, caught in a net with a fine mesh. Civil libertarians who believe that only criminal suspects should ever be subjected to surreptitious surveillance don't give enough weight to intelligence needs.

To decide what if any constitutional rights the little fish have to prevent the government from collecting personal information about them requires making several distinctions. One, noted in Chapter 4, is between information that is merely searched electronically and information that is scrutinized by a human being. An electronic search no more invades privacy than does a dog trained to sniff out illegal drugs, though the dog's "alerting" to the presence of drugs in a container provides probable cause for a (human) investigator to search the container.

Another distinction is between the pure interest in concealment of personal information and the instrumental interest based on fear that the information will be used against one. In many cultures, including our own, there is a nudity taboo. Except in the sex industry (prostitution, striptease, pornography, etc.), nudist colonies, and locker rooms, people generally are embarrassed to be seen naked by strangers, particularly of the opposite sex, even when there are no practical consequences. Why this is so is unclear, but it is a brute fact about the psychology of most people in our society. A woman (an occasional man as well) might be disturbed to learn that nude photographs taken surreptitiously of her had been seen by a stranger in a remote country before being destroyed. That invasion of privacy would not have harmed her in any practical sense. Yet it might cause her at least transitory emotional distress, and that is a harm even if it has no rational basis. But if the stranger used the photos to blackmail her, or in an effort to destroy her budding career as an anchorwoman for the Christian Broadcasting System published the photos in *Hustler* magazine, she would have a different and stronger grievance.

Of course, in many cases of instrumental concealment of personal information the motive is disreputable (deceptive, manipulative): a person might want to conceal his age or a serious health problem from a prospective spouse, or his criminal record from a prospective employer. But not in all cases; the blackmailed woman in my example was not trying to mislead anyone in resisting the publication of the photos.

Legitimate deliberative activity, another example of legitimate instrumental concealment, can be deterred by publicity, because publicity hampers candid communication. When people are speaking freely they say things that an eavesdropping stranger is likely to misconstrue. When they speak guardedly because they are afraid that a stranger is listening in, the clarity and candor of their communication to the intended recipients are impaired. There is a social value in frank communications, including being able to try out ideas on friends or colleagues without immediate exposure to attacks from rivals or ill-wishers. Legitimate strategic plans also require secrecy to be effective. Competition would be greatly undermined if business firms could eavesdrop on competitors' planning sessions or steal their trade secrets with impunity. And, as the Supreme Court recognized in *NAACP v. Alabama ex rel. Patterson* (1957), freedom of political speech requires allowing a controversial advocacy group, whose members if known might be exposed to retaliation, to keep its membership list secret. Government, too, is a site of deliberations, and therefore has a legitimate interest in a degree of privacy. Civil libertarians want government to be transparent but private individuals to be opaque; national security hawks want the reverse. People hide from the government, and government hides from the people, and both the people and the government have both good and bad reasons for hiding from the other. Complete transparency paralyzes planning and action; complete opacity endangers both liberty and security. Terrorists know this best. Eavesdropping imposes costs on innocent people because their privacy is compromised, but the costs it imposes on terrorists are even steeper because it thwarts their plans utterly and places them at risk of capture or death. Of course, from our standpoint as a people endangered by terrorism, the higher those costs the better.

Many people are frightened of the eavesdropping capacity of modern electronic technology. Suppose that the National Security Agency's listening devices gathered the entire world's electronic communications traffic, digitized it, and stored it in databases, where it was machine-searched for clues to terrorist activity, but the search programs were designed to hide from intelligence officers all data that contained no clues to terrorist plans or activity. The data vacuumed up by the NSA in the first, gathering stage of the intelligence project would after being screened by the search programs present intelligence officers with two types of communication to study: communications that contained innocent references to terrorism, and communications among the terrorists themselves. Both types of communication would be discouraged once people realized the scope of the agency's program, but the consequences for the nation would be critically different. Discouraging innocent people from mentioning anything that might lead a computer search to earmark the communication for examination by an intelligence officer would inhibit the free exchange of ideas on matters of public as well as private importance. But discouraging terrorists from communicating by electronic means would discourage terrorism. Foreign terrorists would find it difficult to communicate with colleagues or sympathizers in the United States if they had to do so face-to-face or through messengers because they knew the government was eavesdropping on all their electronic communications. This is simply my earlier point writ large: protected communications are valuable to the persons communicating, whether they are good people or bad people, and this duality is the source of both the costs and the benefits of intercepting communications for intelligence purposes.

A distinction at once crucial and problematic is between the involuntary and the voluntary disclosure of personal information. The former is illustrated by surreptitious interception of mail, of phone conversations, and of other communications; here the Fourth Amendment comes into play and offers a measure of constitutional protection of privacy (how great a measure I will discuss shortly). Surveillance cameras that photograph pedestrians, a security measure implemented on a huge scale in London (enabling identification of the July 2005 terrorist bombers), is another example, at least if the existence or location of the cameras is concealed. If the entire city is known to be under camera surveillance, the surveillance is no longer surreptitious; submission to it is as a practical matter involuntary.

A far greater amount of personal information is revealed voluntarily than involuntarily, as these words are conventionally used. But the case of the pervasive surveillance cameras, avoidable only by never leaving one's home or by moving to another city, suggests that the distinction is often tenuous. No one is required to drive and therefore to have a driver's license. But driving is a practical necessity for most adult Americans, and if you want to drive legally you need a license, which requires that you disclose certain personal information to the motor vehicle bureau. A federal statute forbids colleges and other educational institutions to reveal a student's grades without his consent. Yet virtually all students give their consent because otherwise a prospective employer is likely to assume the worst. To get a good job, to get health and life insurance, to get a bank loan, to get a credit card, you need to reveal personal information. Every time you make a purchase other than for cash you convey information about your tastes, interests, and income that may well end up in some easily accessible database. Every time you use E-ZPass or some equivalent automatic toll system, your location is recorded. Digitizing medical records will help doctors and patients by making it much easier, swifter, and cheaper to transfer these records when a patient switches doctors or is treated by a new doctor in an emergency or needs to consult a specialist. But once the records are digitized rather than existing solely in the form of hard copies in the office of the patient's primary physician, the risk that unauthorized persons will gain access to them is increased. Nevertheless, the movement to digitize medical records is inexorable.

The reductio ad absurdum would be to argue that since you don't have to have a phone, if the government announces that it is going to tap all phones and you continue using your phone, you have "voluntarily" disclosed the content of your calls to the government. That is a bad argument, but not if the issue is government access to digitized medical records even if the government *required* all medical records to be digitized and sharable over the Internet. That measure would have a justification unrelated to a desire to snoop; in addition, the disclosure of medical information to the doctor in the first place, the information that goes into the records, is voluntary.

An intermediate example would be a law requiring that all homes and offices contain surveillance cameras that would film the interiors continuously, but the government could obtain the films only if it had probable cause to believe that criminal activity had occurred that the cameras had recorded. In the case of homes, at least, such a law would be regarded as an intolerable invasion of privacy. Round-the-clock surveillance, if only by a machine, is felt as an invasion of seclusion in a way that monitoring only communications is not. There are interesting cultural differences. European countries have much stricter laws than the United States does against the acquisition of personal information by business firms, and much laxer laws against the acquisition of personal information by government. The difference reflects American suspicion of government and European suspicion of markets.

But the essential point is that a person would have to be a hermit to be able to function in our society without disclosing a vast amount of personal information to a vast array of public and private demanders. This has long been true, but until recently the information that people voluntarily disclosed to vendors, licensing bureaus, hospitals, and so on was scattered, fugitive (because the bulkiness of paper records usually causes them to be discarded as soon as they lose their value to the enterprise), and searchable only with great difficulty—which provided a further incentive to discard information. So although one had voluntarily disclosed private information on innumerable occasions to sundry recipients, one retained as a practical matter a great deal of privacy. But with digitization, not only can recorded information be retained indefinitely at little cost, but the information held by different merchants, insurers, and government agencies can readily be pooled, opening the way to assembling all the recorded information concerning an individual in a single digital file that can easily be retrieved and searched. It should soon be possible—maybe it is already possible—to create a comprehensive electronic dossier for the vast majority of American adults, the sort of dossier the FBI compiles when it conducts a background investigation of an applicant for sensitive government employment or investigates a criminal suspect. The difference is that the digitized dossier would be continuously updated.

The personal information that an organization collects in the course of its dealings with its customers and employees often has commercial value to another organization as well, to which the collector might therefore like to sell the information. Through such transactions, expanding pools of personal information about individuals are created. The rational seller will, it is true, balance the profit from such a sale against the cost in loss of customers. Many people are reluctant to provide personal information to a supplier, an insurer, or other organization without a contractual assurance that the information will not be resold, and so such assurances are common.

Still, a vast amount of personal information is exchanged and pooled because much information is in official records that the public is legally entitled to inspect (such as registries of title to real estate and most court records, including records of bankruptcy proceedings, often rich in personal information), or because it has found its way onto the Web or was disclosed accidentally or deliberately despite a promise not to disclose it, or because the customer had failed to obtain a promise of confidentiality. Also, digitized information tends to have many more loci than paper documents, residing as it usually will in a number of different computers to which many persons may have access—including hackers. Living a normal American life, one cannot avoid disclosing to strangers a tremendous amount of personal information that will find its way into publicly accessible, readily searchable databases, and so one's privacy, or much of it, is blown.

Yet the Supreme Court has held, in *United States v. Miller* (1976) and other cases, that once a person "voluntarily" reveals personal information to a bank, a health insurer, or any other nonintimate, he loses any constitutional right to claim that his privacy has been invaded should the government obtain the information from the entity to which he had revealed it or an entity to which the receiver had disclosed it. Indeed, earlier the Court had held that even disclosing incriminating information to an undercover agent whom one considered a friend or a trustworthy business associate resulted in the forfeit of any claim to informational privacy. Nothing is more common, moreover, than for a prisoner to snitch on his cellmate; often he will be offered inducements by the authorities to do so. The cellmate whose informational privacy is invaded has no remedy.

It is unclear whether in allowing such tactics the Supreme Court is being unrealistic about the voluntary character of such disclosures (is a disclosure meaningfully "voluntary" when it is procured by deceit?) or believes that the only constitutional protection of informational privacy is found in the Fourth Amendment and that information you reveal in the ordinary course of your personal and business dealings cannot be thought the product of a "search." That is an unsatisfactory explanation because the search occurs not at the initial disclosure but later, when the government demands the information from the bank, insurer, cellmate, or other recipient.

The *Miller* decision is the constitutional foundation of the FBI's "national security letters." These are demands on banks and other records custodians for information that has been voluntarily disclosed to them. If the demand is refused—which is rare, as most custodians want to remain in the Bureau's good graces—the government must ask a court to subpoena the records. There is no constitutional obstacle to the enforcement of such a subpoena. But a court can refuse to enforce it if it is unduly burdensome or invades privacy beyond what seems reasonable (for a pertinent example, see the *Northwestern Memorial Hospital* case [2004]). This limitation on enforcement, ignored by critics of the national security letters, is important because it can be invoked even when information bearing on national security is sought. But it is not a constitutional limitation. A subpoenaed bookstore cannot claim that its record of customers' purchases is constitutionally protected property. The store is merely a repository of information that, having been furnished to it voluntarily, lost the constitutional protection that information receives when seized by the government without consent, as by surreptitious wiretapping. Besides the principles governing the enforcement of a subpoena seeking private information, there is a common-law right of privacy and a number of federal and state privacy statutes—all attesting to the value that people place on their privacy—but they are not directly relevant to my discussion, which is limited to constitutional issues. They do confirm, however, that privacy of information is a highly valued commodity, perhaps one that should be accorded the status of constitutional "property" or "liberty."

CIVIL LIBERTARIANS' CONCERN with the government's demanding access to data found in databases to which individuals have "voluntarily" consigned personal information has focused on section 215 of the USA PATRIOT Act (passed by overwhelming majorities in both houses of Congress within weeks after the 9/11 attacks), and more recently on the collection activities of the National Security Agency in arguable violation of the Foreign Intelligence Surveillance Act. As amended in March 2006, section 215, the so-called (and misnamed) libraries provision, empowers the government to demand books, papers, records, and other materials from any individual or organization (libraries are not singled out, though they are not excluded) if there are reasonable grounds to believe that the records contain information relevant to a national security investigation.

Civil libertarians argue that the government ought to be required to demonstrate that it has a reasonable basis for believing that the person to whom the records pertain is involved in terrorist activity. But as should be clear by now, that would be too restrictive a requirement. To impose it would be either to misunderstand the needs of intelligence or to underestimate the value of intelligence in the struggle against terrorism (or perhaps to underestimate the terrorist threat). Information about an individual who is *not* part of a terrorist ring may nevertheless be highly germane to an investigation of the ring or, what may be as important, to an investigation aimed at discovering the existence of such rings. The information might concern an imam who, though not himself involved in terrorism, was preaching holy war. It might concern family members of a terrorist, who might have information about his whereabouts. It might consist of sales invoices for materials that could be used to create weapons of mass destruction, or of books and articles that expressed admiration for suicide bombers.

The impact of section 215 on civil liberties is quite limited—only a few dozen section 215 demands have been served on libraries. Most records custodians will, as I said, voluntarily hand over nonprivileged records to the government when told the records may contain information relevant to national security. A custodian's refusal to disclose the records might generate enough suspicion to enable the government to obtain a subpoena even under a much narrower version of section 215.

One understands, though, why civil libertarians have labeled section 215 the "libraries provision" despite its being used so rarely against libraries. To discover what people have been reading, as distinct from discovering their financial or health status, is to gain insight into what they are thinking—and what they are planning. This is *why* the government might want to obtain a record of a person's library borrowings (not to mention his bookstore purchases, records of which also fall within the scope of section 215). And when the quest for knowledge of what a person is thinking is driven by concern with terrorism, which is almost always politically motivated, success in the quest is likely to include the acquisition of a comprehensive picture of the subject's political beliefs. Knowing that the government is seeking to compile such pictures, people of unorthodox views may hesitate to buy or borrow books that express such views. This is the same issue that is raised by the government's conducting surveillance of mosques. Whether such surveillance presents Fourth Amendment problems depends on the method used to conduct it; surveillance as such, as we saw in Chapter 4, does not violate the First Amendment despite its undoubted effect on the exercise of free speech.

The *Miller* line of decisions, in holding that a voluntary disclosure of information manifests a willingness to waive or forfeit any right of privacy, seems unrealistic about the meaning not only of "voluntary" but also of "privacy" itself. Informational privacy does not mean refusing to share information with everyone. Obviously a telephone conversation is not private in that sense, nor a letter, nor a conversation between spouses or friends. Every conversation is at least two-sided. The fact that I disclose symptoms of illness to my doctor does not make my health a public fact, especially if he promises (or the rules of the medical profession require him) not to disclose my medical history to anyone without my permission.

One must not confuse solitude with secrecy; they are distinct forms of privacy. Solitude fosters individualistic attitudes; conversely, the constant presence of other people or the sense of being under constant surveillance enforces conformity. But one also needs freedom to communicate in private. The planning of organized activity obviously is impossible without communication; less obviously, productive independent thinking almost always requires bouncing ideas off other people. And few of us are sufficiently independent-minded to persist in an unorthodox idea if we don't discover that others share it.

If "liberty" in the Fifth Amendment's due process clause can connote sexual freedom, and "due process" can be understood to require that any restriction on liberty be no greater than is necessary, why can't there be a due process right to control information about oneself that is not already public knowledge, unless one is trying to use that control for unlawful ends or the government has a pressing need for the information? Maybe there can be—provided, however, that the "pressing need" qualification is taken seriously. Constitutional rights, as we have seen throughout this book, are not absolutes whose scope is fixed without regard to competing interests. How much information about oneself one should be permitted to withhold from the government depends critically on how valuable the information is to the government. In an era of global terrorism and proliferation of weapons of mass destruction, the government has a compelling need to gather, pool, sift, and search vast quantities of information, much of it personal.

I SAID AT THE OUTSET of this chapter that Americans value their privacy; here I add that they value two aspects of privacy the most. The first is being free to go about one's business with a minimum of interference; the second is not having personal facts used against one. The latter is a subset of what I have been calling the secrecy sense of privacy. Americans are not known for reticence or personal modesty. Most of us are quite casual about disclosing personal information to strangers, provided it isn't likely to boomerang. The widespread use of that most indiscreet of communications media, the Internet, is not the only evidence of this. People have become blasé about having their personal belongings X-rayed and their persons searched by security personnel at airports. They are overheard everywhere talking loudly on cell phones. They are oblivious to the mushrooming of surveillance cameras, interior as well as exterior. Fewer people make use of encryption programs to conceal their electronic communications than invite strangers to read their correspondence: Gmail, Google's e-mail application, automatically searches the text of an e-mail and posts advertisements keyed to its content. Gmail is immensely popular.

The fact that one can't negotiate modernity without continuously revealing personal information to a variety of demanders has resulted in a lowering of expectations of privacy. People have become habituated to a culture of radically diminished informational privacy. In this new culture, the degree to which a disclosure of personal information inflicts harm depends less on what information is disclosed than to whom, and to how many, and what use it is put to by people to whom it is disclosed. Maybe most of us no longer care much if strangers know intimate details of our private lives, though this depends on who the strangers are and whether the details that each possesses are combined to create a comprehensive dossier on us.

Intelligence officials like to say that the information they're interested in is actually more limited than the information that a medical provider or public health officer, a prospective spouse or employer, a health or life insurer, or even a bank or other seller of goods or services would like to have. That is both correct and incorrect. In the initial computer sifting designed to pick out data meriting scrutiny by an intelligence officer, only facts bearing on national security will trigger scrutiny. But once an individual is identified as a possible terrorist or foreign agent, the government's interest in him will explode. Besides obtaining contact information, it will want to learn about his ethnicity and national origin, education and skills, previous addresses and travel (especially overseas), family, friends and acquaintances, political and religious beliefs and activities, finances, any arrest or other criminal record, military service if any, mental health and other psychological attributes, and a range of consumption activities, the whole adding up to a comprehensive personal profile. If these profiles are digitized, pooled, and searched electronically to reveal links and interactions among individuals, the intelligence services will have access to a body of information of potentially very great utility for identifying and tracking members of terrorist cells and piecing together their financial and other support networks. They will, for example, know everything that Amazon.com knows about an individual's preferences in books and movies because they will have gotten the information from Amazon.com, and they will know a great deal more by pooling that information with information from other sources, public and private.

I mentioned this kind of national security data gathering in Chapter 4, but here I want to emphasize the degree to which it would *not* depend on electronic surveillance that would raise questions under the Fourth Amendment or under statutes such as Title III (the general federal wiretap statute) and the Foreign Intelligence Surveillance Act. The Defense Department's Able Danger project (well discussed in an article by Shane Harris) showed that valuable intelligence could be obtained without the kind of surveillance that normally requires a warrant.

Privacy is the terrorist's best friend, and the terrorist's privacy has been enhanced by the same technological developments that have both made data mining feasible and elicited vast quantities of personal information from innocents: anonymity combined with the secure encryption of digitized data makes the Internet a powerful tool of conspiracy. The government has a compelling need to exploit digitization in defense of national security. But if this is permitted, intelligence officers are going to be scrutinizing a mass of personal information about U.S. citizens. And we know that people don't like even complete strangers poring over the details of their private lives. But the fewer of these strangers who have access to those details and the more professional their interest in them, the less the affront to privacy. One reason people don't much mind having their bodies examined by doctors is that they know that doctors' interest in bodies is professional rather than prurient; we can hope that the same is true of intelligence professionals.

The primary danger of such data mining is leaks by intelligence personnel to persons inside or outside the government who might use the leaked data for improper purposes. Information collected by a national security data-mining program would have to be sharable within the national security community, which would include in appropriate cases foreign intelligence services, but not beyond. Severe sanctions and other security measures (encryption, restricted access, etc.) could and should be imposed in order to prevent—realistically, to minimize—the leakage of such information outside the community. My suggestion in the last chapter that the principle of the Pentagon Papers case be relaxed to permit measures to prevent the media from publishing properly classified information would reinforce protection of the privacy of information obtained by national security data mining.

I have said both that people value their informational privacy and that they surrender it at the drop of a hat. The paradox is resolved by noting that as long as people don't expect that the details of their health, love life, or finances will be used to harm them in their interactions with other people, they are content to reveal those details to strangers when they derive benefits from the revelation. As long as intelligence personnel can be trusted to use their knowledge of such details only for the defense of the nation, the public will be compensated for the costs of diminished privacy in increased security from terrorist attacks.

Civil libertarians will not be reassured. They combine an instinctive distrust of government activities to protect national security with a systematic disparagement of the menace to national security that terrorists pose. The distrust is excessive and the disparagement irresponsible. Although there is a history of misuse by the FBI, the CIA, and local police forces of personal information collected ostensibly for law enforcement and intelligence purposes, it is not a recent history. The legal and bureaucratic controls over such misuse are much tighter than they used to be, in part because of the investigations conducted by the Church and Pike committees in the 1970s. The media are nosier, more vigilant, more competitive. Whistleblowers have more legal protection against retaliation. Legal sanctions on misconduct by government officials are heavier. The new criminal-investigative technique of interrogating journalists about the sources of the leaks they publish, such as the leak of the identity of Valerie Plame Wilson as an undercover CIA officer—a breach of privacy—will reduce the number of leaks. The point is not that human nature has changed since the days when J. Edgar Hoover ran roughshod over civil liberties; it hasn't. It's the environment in which law enforcement and intelligence personnel work that has changed, reducing the risk of abuse of private information by its governmental custodians at the same time that the menace of terrorism has increased. The lines have crossed.

. . .

Conclusion

CONSTITUTIONAL RIGHTS are largely created by the Supreme Court, by loose interpretation of the constitutional text. Created as they are in response to the felt needs and conditions of the time, they can be and frequently are modified by the Court in response to changes in those needs and conditions. A constitutional right *should* be modified when changed circumstances indicate that the right no longer strikes a sensible balance between competing constitutional values, such as personal liberty and public safety. A national emergency, such as a war, creates a disequilibrium in the existing system of constitutional rights. Concerns for public safety now weigh more heavily than before. The courts respond by altering the balance, curtailing civil liberties in recognition that the relative weights of the competing interests have changed in favor of safety. That is the pragmatic response, and pragmatism is a dominant feature not only of American culture at large but also of the American judicial culture.

What the current administration calls the "war on terrorism" is not a conventional war, because it is not a military conflict with a foreign state. But it has essential features of a war, indeed of a total war. It is a violent conflict with a powerful, resilient enemy that wants to injure the United States and Europe grievously, overthrow governments in the Middle East, Africa, and Central and Southeast Asia, destroy Israel, and force the United States to withdraw from the Eastern Hemisphere. Al-Qaeda and its spin-offs and allies constitute a formidable enemy. Their lack of a national base makes them in some ways more dangerous than when they had one in Afghanistan because it weakens our ability to retaliate against them or even find them. The stakes are magnified by the enemy's effort to obtain and deploy weapons of mass destruction, which are becoming increasingly accessible to terrorist groups and against which, in the hands of terrorists, retaliation in kind is impossible. The fighting is intermittent (except in Iraq), but that is a feature of many wars.

We have enemies besides the terrorists. But it is the peculiarly insidious character of the terrorist threat that requires responsive measures that test our commitment to civil liberties and make the question of the constitutional balance between liberty and safety an urgent one. With the 9/11 attacks receding in time, forgetfulness and complacency are becoming the order of the day. Are we safer today or do we just feel safer? Though scattered by our invasion of Afghanistan and by our stepped-up efforts at counterterrorism, terrorist leaders may even now be regrouping, and preparing an attack that will produce destruction on a scale to dwarf 9/11.

I have argued that the proper way to think about constitutional rights in a time such as this is in terms of the metaphor of a balance. One pan contains individual rights, the other community safety, with the balance needing and receiving readjustment from time to time as the weights of the respective interests change. The safer we feel, the more weight we place on the interest in personal liberty; the more endangered we feel, the more weight we place on the interest in safety, while recognizing the interdependence of the two interests. Civil libertarians should value safety not only for its intrinsic merits but also because a terrorist attack or other national security crisis incites curtailments of civil liberties. National security experts should value civil liberties not only for their intrinsic value, and not only because civil liberties abuses could cause disaffection among members of communities whose loyalty to the nation is at once vital and perhaps precarious, but also because civil liberties reinforce the separation of powers by limiting the discretion of the executive branch. The separation of powers is an essential mechanism for correcting the errors to which each branch of government would be prone in the absence of a competitive environment.

Civil liberties and constitutional rights tend to be discussed in the same breath, but they are not synonyms. Civil liberties are shaped by statutes, regulations, and the discretionary judgments of law enforcement and national security personnel as well as by courts in the name of the Constitution. Prudential and practical considerations, as well as public opinion (including elite public opinion, which is often highly influential with Congress) and interest group pressures, have resulted in the creation by legislatures and courts of a body of statutory and common-law civil liberties that is far more extensive than anything to be found in the text or the authoritative interpretations of the Constitution. I noted in Chapter 3 how the right of a U.S. citizen detained as an enemy combatant to seek habeas corpus was confirmed by the Supreme Court on the basis of a statute, and in Chapter 4 how FISA was a legislative reaction (indeed overreaction) to executive-branch abuses. Recall too how the House of Representatives defied public opinion by impeaching President Clinton. Congress has a mind of its own—it is not just a transmitter of ignorant public opinion, let alone a toady of the executive branch. This point reinforces what should be the cornerstone of judicial interpretation of the Constitution in emergency situations, which is judicial modesty. The Supreme Court's constitutional decisions are extremely difficult to change except by the Court itself, which is, however, reluctant to overrule its decisions lest by doing so it acknowledge the essentially pragmatic, political, and ad hoc character of constitutional decision making. And Supreme Court justices have scant knowledge of national security, a deficiency that may make them lean too far either way—in favor of what they do understand, which is the legal tradition of protecting civil liberties, or in favor of upholding security measures because they don't understand them. Congress knows more about national security and so may perform a more effective checking function on the president than the courts are able to do.

It is a matter of concern when the legal cart is put before the policy horse, so that instead of asking the practical question of what should be done, we ask the lawyers what their partial and parochial perspective, their traditions and hobbyhorses, their shibboleths and taboos, their rights fetishes, and their imagined histories lead them to recommend. Consider once again the storm that arose in December 2005 over the president's having ordered the National Security Agency to conduct electronic surveillance outside the framework created by the Foreign Intelligence Surveillance Act. The critics charged that the surveillance violated the act, as indeed it seemed to. The administration riposted that the joint resolution authorizing force against al-Qaeda, viewed as a declaration of war, was an implicit authorization of whatever surveillance the commander in chief might think necessary to the prosecution of the war and that anyway the president, as commander in chief, cannot be straitjacketed in his conduct of war by a mere statute. The administration also argued that the warrant procedure imposed by FISA is too cumbersome. Even though the warrant can be sought retroactively (up to seventy-two hours after the surveillance begins) if there is no time to get it in advance, the sheer volume of modern communications makes it difficult to cope with the paperwork burdens of literal compliance with the statute; the statute requires that the warrant application contain a formidable amount of information. Critics argued that if FISA is unworkable in the era of global terrorism and advanced communications, it should be amended, not flouted or bypassed. All this legal cut-and-thrust was premature. The focus of debate should have been on the adequacy of FISA in the current emergency. If it is inadequate—and it surely is—it can be changed (as civil libertarians point out) or perhaps bypassed (as the administration argued).

When the question is cast as one of constitutional rights and powers, the priority of policy analysis over legal analysis is even more imperative. Constitutional law is especially plastic, for reasons discussed in the first chapter of this book. Intuitions of policy guide the judges in molding the plastic into some definite shape. Policy, together with such institutional or systemic concerns as the competence of judges to evaluate national security needs and the proper balance between the judiciary and the other branches of government (judicial activism versus judicial modesty or self-restraint), should be the focus of debate over how far the Constitution should be understood to limit government responses to national emergencies.

Analysis guided by these concerns has persuaded me that the measures taken in the wake of the 9/11 attacks to combat the terrorist threat do not violate the Constitution, except the effort to deny the right of habeas corpus to U.S. citizens—a measure that the Supreme Court invalidated—and to foreign terrorist suspects captured in the United States. Terrorist suspects are entitled to due process of law, but they can be tried as unlawful combatants before military tribunals (the constitutionality of which is at this writing pending in the Supreme Court) and thus denied most of the constitutional rights possessed by criminal defendants. Additional counterterrorist measures, in particular in the related areas of electronic surveillance and computerized data mining, could be taken without violating the Constitution (even if there were a clear constitutional right to informational privacy), especially if the effect on privacy is minimized by a strict rule against using information obtained through such means for any purpose other than to protect national security. More can be done to deter the leaking of national security secrets to the media and, if necessary (I do not think it is yet necessary), to crack down on extremist speech. Coercive interrogation up to and including torture might survive constitutional challenge as long as the fruits of such interrogation were not used in a criminal prosecution. I repeat that the Constitution is not the sum total of civil liberties. Statutes and treaties provide additional protections. Constitutional law is a looser garment, continually rewoven by Supreme Court justices mindful (one hopes) of the need to balance security and liberty concerns as the weights of these concerns shift.

I want to close by returning to an earlier theme that requires qualifying the metaphor of the balance. Recall the discussion in Chapter 4 of whether it is better to have a strict legal rule against torture and hope that it will be violated in situations of genuine exigency or to recognize in the formulation of the constitutional principle itself that torture should be permitted in truly exigent circumstances. The general question is whether to govern difficult and sensitive issues that arise at the intersection of civil liberties and national security by a rule or by a standard. Although legal principles should be based on a balancing of competing interests, it is a separate question whether to embody the balance in a rule or in a standard. The former will be simpler to enforce, but its application is likely to produce occasional anomalies. The latter will avoid the anomalies but by its inherent sponginess invite applications that may distort its scope.

Rules create a space for what might be termed "licensed civil disobedience." To stop up any loopholes, they characteristically are overinclusive. If they are legal rules, they overstate duties, with the further aim of repelling cynicism and "making a statement." No one actually goes through life never violating the letter of the law; "work to rule" is a well-known method of industrial sabotage, as activity grinds to a halt unless work rules are bent from time to time. So in practice many violations of rules, including legal rules, are condoned, and even approved, though usually tacitly in order to preserve the rules. The combination of an overinclusive rule with prosecutorial discretion (that is, authority not to prosecute even a clear violation of law) may be superior in many situations both to a standard and to a rule that is festooned with exceptions. The upshot is a class of criminal acts that are not excused but are nevertheless permitted. It is a long-standing device of government that should not be scorned.

There is even a sense, though it is easily misunderstood, in which rules are made to be broken. The choice to govern some activity by a rule is a choice to exclude from consideration some relevant circumstances in the interest of clarity and simplicity. But those circumstances do not cease to be relevant; they hover in the wings, as it were, waiting for a case to arise in which their force is so great that the rule must bend, either by recognition of a new exception or by simply being ignored.

Lincoln was morally justified in suspending habeas corpus at the outset of the Civil War, not only because there was strong support for the Confederacy in key states, notably Maryland (which together with Virginia surrounds the District of Columbia), but also and relatedly because the Union was in grave peril. To prevent a collapse of the North's will to fight, Lincoln had to demonstrate unflinching resolve to resist the secession, and one way to do that was to act sternly against disloyal citizens. The importance of demonstrating resolve at the outset of a grim struggle explains and to a degree justifies the excesses of repression that so often accompany our entry into war, including the war against al-Qaeda.

One response to Lincoln's actions might be to say that if he was acting justifiably, we should amend the Constitution to authorize presidents to suspend habeas corpus in emergencies (or at least ask Congress to authorize the president to suspend habeas corpus, a measure arguably within Congress's suspension power, though remember that the power is limited, perhaps too narrowly, to cases of invasion or rebellion). The alternative, which has been chosen by default, is to say that we are not going to give the president that legal authority but we are going to expect him to suspend habeas corpus if doing so is necessary (as Lincoln believed) to save the nation. I prefer the latter approach; the fact that it has worked pretty well for more than two centuries is a practical argument for its retention.

A president legally authorized to suspend habeas corpus in an emergency would be tempted to test the outer bounds of "emergency" (or whatever other formula was chosen to define his suspension authority) because presidents want to expand their power. If the legal authority is withheld, the president will be cautious in his definition of an emergency, since if the exigent need to violate the Constitution is not plain he will pay a high political price for his illegal action, as Nixon did. To put this differently, conferring legal authority to suspend constitutional rights reduces the cost of that extreme action to the president, and we may want him to bear a heavy (though not prohibitively heavy) cost so that he will be temperate in his exercise of power. There is the further concern that if the suspension power is narrowly defined it will fail to make provision for novel emergencies (notice how Congress's authority to suspend habeas corpus, being limited to situations of rebellion or invasion, fits poorly with the emergency created by the 9/11 attacks—were they an "invasion"?), while if it is broadly defined it will give the president too much power.

In a curious way, the extralegal approach that I am defending places tighter constraints on the president than the legal approach of amending the Constitution to authorize suspending constitutional rights in emergencies, and is structurally more akin to the preferred approach of civil libertarians. They like rules that are protective of civil liberties and allow for only narrow exceptions. My approach has the rule-and-exception structure, but the only exceptions are the ad hoc ones that presidents "buy" by paying the political price of breaking the law. In contrast, legal authorization for suspending constitutional rights in emergencies would operate in practice as a loose standard within whose capacious and perhaps elastic bounds the president could operate without paying any political price.

An intermediate approach deserves some consideration. It would be to extend the doctrine of "qualified immunity," which allows a public officer to escape having to pay damages for an illegal act that he has committed if the illegality was not clearly established when he acted, to national security officials who violate a constitutional right in good faith in compelling situations of necessity. In the famous English case of *Regina v. Dudley & Stevens* (1884) the defendants, adrift on the open sea in a lifeboat after their ship sank, killed and ate the third person in the boat, a cabin boy. The cabin boy was dying, and all three probably would have died had the defendants not resorted to cannibalism. The defendants were nevertheless prosecuted for murder, convicted, sentenced to death—and immediately pardoned. That was an ad hoc response evoked by reluctance to try to define a defense of "reasonable cannibalism." I am suggesting something more systematic—a partial defense in cases in which a rule is violated in extraordinary circumstances. This may be the best approach as we move deeper into the era of international terrorism and weapons of mass destruction. If it is rejected, we can expect a rash of presidential pardons of national security officers; we might even witness the spectacle of a president's pardoning himself, which apparently would be legal (see my book *An Affair of State*).

The partial defense will not always do the trick, even if it is extended to excuse criminal as well as civil liability, because a court may deem the defendant's violation unarguable. That would be a likely response in a case of torture, however compelling the practical argument for it in the particular case—the ticking-time-bomb case that civil libertarians are reluctant to acknowledge, for example. So should we worry that unless we legalize all tactics that might be justified in a national emergency, it will be difficult to find public officers who are willing to assume the legal risk of using them? (The purpose of the qualified immunity defense is indeed to make public officers less timid in the performance of their duties.) I think not. In national emergencies most soldiers and other security personnel are willing to do what the situation demands and leave their legal liabilities to be sorted out later. They live for such emergencies, and they are selected for courage.

A comparative perspective on the question of suspending constitutional rights in an emergency may be illuminating. Despite the sorry precedent of Weimar Germany, most European countries, perhaps all, allow the head of state—the president or the (constitutional) monarch—to exercise such a power; Article 15 of the European Convention on Human Rights authorizes such exercise. This power, which foreign nations vest in the head of state, our Constitution vests in Congress, for the power to suspend habeas corpus is essentially the power to suspend constitutional rights—if you cannot get a judge to hear your case, the government can do whatever it wants with you.

The reason for this difference in where the suspension power is lodged lies in the difference between the parliamentary and presidential systems of government. The former has a head of state who is usually at some distance above the ordinary play of politics (the prime minister is the nation's political leader), and so he can be entrusted with such a power. The U.S. president, however, is at once the head of state and the nation's political leader, and so he is not trusted to exercise such power in a politically disinterested fashion. But the congressional alternative is unsatisfactory too, not only because Congress is a political body but also because it is not designed for taking prompt and decisive action. This makes the extralegal approach to the exercise of emergency powers an attractive alternative in our system.

But there is a downside, noted by Machiavelli in commending (in chapter 34 of the *Discourses*) the provision in the law of the Roman Republic for six-month emergency dictatorships. It is that condoning legal violations by the nation's highest official will bring the laws—the foundation of republican government—into disrepute. (This was the principal ground for the impeachment of President Clinton.) But maybe we can climb out of this box by recognizing, in an echo of Lincoln, a category of "constitutional unconstitutional" actions, as Benjamin Kleinerman urges:

First, action outside and sometimes against the Constitution is only constitutional when the constitutional union itself is at risk; a concern for the public good is insufficient grounds for the executive to exercise discretionary power. Second, the Constitution should be understood as different during extraordinary times than during ordinary times; thus discretionary action should take place only in extraordinary circumstances and should be understood as extraordinary. Since it is only necessitated by the crisis, the action should have no effect on the existing law. To preserve constitutionalism after the crisis, the actions must not be regularized or institutionalized. Third, a line must separate the executive's personal feeling and his official duty. He should take only those actions that fulfill his official duty, the preservation of the Constitution, even, or especially, if the people want him to go further.

However, one can imagine a president treating Kleinerman's three-factor test as a rule and thus wanting to see how far it can be stretched.

We will have less "action outside and sometimes against the Constitution" if we insist that the president's power to disobey the law be acknowledged as power, not authority, and be justified as such rather than sugared over with legalism, as in the ingenious suggestion that the Constitution "should be understood as different during extraordinary times." The Constitution is not different if it is the president who suspends habeas corpus instead of Congress; the president's suspension of it is unconstitutional, and so justification for it must be sought in a "law of necessity" understood not as law but as the trumping of law by necessity, as in the case of rebellion or invasion. There can be such a thing as an excess of legalism, as President Roosevelt recognized when he violated the Neutrality Act in 1940 by supplying munitions to Great Britain to keep it in the war.

Bruce Ackerman, going well beyond Kleinerman, suggests a variety of controls over presidential assumptions of emergency powers, including strict time limits and frequently required reauthorizations by Congress, that deserve consideration as an alternative approach to the law of necessity.

But these are details. The essential point is that, one way or another, law must adjust to necessity born of emergency. In the words of David Hume, an eighteenth-century voice speaking with greater clarity than the Constitution:

> The safety of the people is the supreme law: All other particular laws are subordinate to it, and dependent on it: And if, in the *common* course of things, they be followed and regarded; it is only because the public safety and interest *commonly* demand so equal and impartial an administration.

. . .

Further Readings

BOOKS AND ARTICLES

Ackerman, Bruce. *Before the Next Attack: Preserving Civil Liberties in an Age of Terrorism* (2006).

Ackerman, Spencer. "Religious Protection: Why American Muslims Haven't Turned to Terrorism." *New Republic*, Dec. 12, 2005, 18.

Alschuler, Albert W. "Racial Profiling and the Constitution." 2002 *University of Chicago Legal Forum* 163.

Bickers, John M. "Military Commissions Are Constitutionally Sound: A Response to Professors Katyal and Tribe." 34 *Texas Tech Law Review* 899 (2003).

Blackstone, William. *Commentaries on the Laws of England*, vol. 3, 132–33 (1768); vol. 4, 151–52 (1769).

Breyer, Stephen. *Active Liberty: Interpreting Our Democratic Constitution* (2005).

Cole, David, and James X. Dempsey. *Terrorism and the Constitution: Sacrificing Civil Liberties in the Name of National Security* 181–87 (2002).

The Constitution in Wartime: Beyond Alarmism and Complacency (Mark Tushnet ed. 2005).

Dempsey, James X., and Lara M. Flint. "Commercial Data and National Security." 72 *George Washington Law Review* 1459 (2004).

DeRosa, Mary. "Data Mining and Data Analysis for Counterterrorism." CSIS [Center for Strategic and International Studies], Mar. 2004.

Dershowitz, Alan M. *Preemption: A Knife That Cuts Both Ways* (2006).

———. *Why Terrorism Works* (2003).

Dworkin, Ronald. "The Threat to Patriotism." *New York Review of Books*, Feb. 28, 2002, 44, 47.

Edgar, Harold, and Benno C. Schmidt Jr. "The Espionage Statutes and Publication of Defense Information." 73 *Columbia Law Review* 929 (1973).

Ely, John Hart. *Democracy and Distrust: A Theory of Judicial Review* (1980).

Etzioni, Amitai. "Privacy and Secrecy in Electronic Communications." Chapter 3 of *How Patriotic Is the Patriot Act? Freedom Versus Security in the Age of Terrorism* (2004).

Gross, Oren. "The Prohibition on Torture and the Limits of the Law." In *Torture: A Collection* 229 (Sanford Levinson ed. 2004).

Harris, Shane. "Army Project Illustrates Promise, Shortcomings of Data Mining." GovExec.com, Dec. 7, 2005, http://www.govexec.com/dailyfed/1205/120705nj1.htm.

Heymann, Philip B., and Juliette N. Kayyem. *Protecting Liberty in an Age of Terror* (2005).

Hui, Kai-Lung, and I. P. L. Png. "The Economics of Privacy." *Handbook of Information Systems and Economics* (Terry Hendershott ed. forthcoming).

Hume, David. *An Enquiry Concerning the Principles of Morals* 29 (1777).

Issacharoff, Samuel, and Richard H. Pildes. "Between Civil Libertarianism and Executive Unilateralism: An Institutional Process Approach to Rights During Wartime." In *The Constitution in Wartime: Beyond Alarmism and Complacency* 161 (Mark Tushnet ed. 2005).

Kagan, Elena. "Presidential Power." 114 *Harvard Law Review* 2245 (2001).

Katyal, Neal K., and Laurence H. Tribe. "Waging War, Deciding Guilt: Trying the Military Tribunals." 111 *Yale Law Journal* 1259 (2002).

Kerr, Orin S. "Searches and Seizures in a Digital World." 119 *Harvard Law Review* 531, 576–84 (2005).

Kleinerman, Benjamin A. "Lincoln's Example: Executive Power and the Survival of Constitutionalism." 3 *Perspectives on Politics* 801, 808 (2005).

"Law Professors' Petition to Congress." In David Cole and James X. Dempsey, *Terrorism and the Constitution: Sacrificing Civil Liberties in the Name of National Security* 189, 191–92 (2002).

Luban, David. "Eight Fallacies About Liberty and Security." In *Human Rights in the "War on Terror"* 242, 248 (Richard Ashby Wilson ed. 2005).

Moore, John Norton, and Robert F. Turner. *National Security Law* (2d ed. 2005).

Moynihan, Daniel Patrick. *Secrecy: The American Experience* (1998).

Patriot Debates: Experts Debate the USA PATRIOT Act (Stewart A. Baker and John Kavanagh eds. 2005).

Posner, Eric A., and Adrian Vermeule. "Accommodating Emergencies." In *The Constitution in Wartime: Beyond Alarmism and Complacency* 55 (Mark Tushnet ed. 2005).

———. "Emergencies and Democratic Failure." University of Chicago Law School, 2005.

———. *Terror in the Balance: Security, Liberty, and the Courts.* Forthcoming.

Posner, Richard A. *Uncertain Shield: The U.S. Intelligence System in the Throes of Reform* 129–39 (2006).

———. "The Supreme Court 2004 Term: Foreword: A Political Court." 119 *Harvard Law Review* 31 (2005).

———. *Preventing Surprise Attacks: Intelligence Reform in the Wake of 9/11* 182–96 (2005).

———. *Catastrophe: Risk and Response* 224–45 (2004).

———. *Law, Pragmatism, and Democracy* 293–317 (2003).

———. *An Affair of State: The Investigation, Impeachment, and Trial of President Clinton* (1999).

———. "Privacy and Related Interests." Part 3 of *The Economics of Justice* (1981).

Schauer, Frederick. "Fear, Risk and the First Amendment: Unraveling the 'Chilling Effect.'" 58 *Boston University Law Review* 685 (1978).

Sheffer, Martin S. "Presidential Power to Suspend Habeas Corpus: The Taney-Bates Dialogue and Ex Parte Merryman." 11 *Oklahoma City University Law Review* 1, 23 (1986).

Solove, Daniel J. "Fourth Amendment Codification and Professor Kerr's Misguided Call for Judicial Deference." 74 *Fordham Law Review* 747 (2005).

———. "A Taxonomy of Privacy," 154 *University of Pennsylvania Law Review* 477 (2006).

Stone, Geoffrey R. *Perilous Times: Free Speech in Wartime: From the Sedition Act of 1798 to the War on Terrorism* (2004).

Taylor, Stuart Jr. "Decommission the Commissions," *Atlantic Monthly*, April, 2006.

Terrorism in Context (Martha Crenshaw ed. 1995).

Terrorism, the Laws of War, and the Constitution: Debating the Enemy Combatant Cases (Peter Berkowitz ed. 2005).

Torture: A Collection (Sanford Levinson ed. 2004).

Waldron, Jeremy. "Torture and the Positive Law: Jurisprudence for the White House." 105 *Columbia Law Review* 1681 (2005).

———. "Security and Liberty: The Image of Balance." 11 *Journal of Political Philosophy* 191 (2003).

Warren, Samuel D., and Louis D. Brandeis. "The Right to Privacy." 4 *Harvard Law Review* 193 (1890).

Woods, Michael J. "Counterintelligence and Access to Transactional Records: A Practical History of USA PATRIOT Act Section 215." 1 *Journal of National Security Law & Policy* 37 (2005).

Yoo, John. *The Powers of War and Peace: The Constitution and Foreign Affairs After 9/11* (2005).

COURT CASES

Alliance to End Repression v. City of Chicago, 742 F.2d 1007, 1015–6 (7th Cir. 1984) (en banc).

Alliance to End Repression v. City of Chicago, 237 F.3d 799, 801–2 (7th Cir. 2001).

Bartnicki v. Vopper, 532 U.S. 514, 529–30 (2001).

Brandenburg v. Ohio, 395 U.S. 444, 447 (1969) (per curiam).

Carpenter v. United States, 484 U.S. 19 (1987).

City of Indianapolis v. Edmond, 531 U.S. 32, 45 (2000).

Cunningham v. Neagle, 135 U.S. 1, 64 (1890).

Dennis v. United States, 341 U.S. 494 (1951).

Ex parte Merryman, 17 Fed. Cas. 144 (Cir. Ct. D. Md. 1861).

Ex parte Milligan, 71 U.S. 2 (1866).

Ex parte Quirin, 317 U.S. 1 (1942).

Florida v. J.L., 529 U.S. 266, 273–74 (2000).

Hamdi v. Rumsfeld, 542 U.S. 507 (2004).

Illinois v. Lidster, 540 U.S. 419 (2004).

In re Sealed Case, 310 F.3d 717 (U.S. Foreign Intelligence Surveillance Court of Review 2002).

In re Yamashita, 327 U.S. 1 (1946).

Johnson v. Eisentrager, 339 U.S. 763 (1950).

Keith. See *United States v. United States District Court*.

Kennedy v. Mendoza-Martinez, 372 U.S. 144, 160 (1963).

Korematsu v. United States, 323 U.S. 214 (1944).

NAACP v. Alabama ex rel. Patterson, 357 U.S. 449, 462–63 (1957)

New York Times Co. v. United States, 403 U.S. 713 (1971) (per curiam).

Northwestern Memorial Hospital v. Ashcroft, 362 F.3d 923 (7th Cir. 2004).

Olmstead v. United States, 277 U.S. 438 (1928).

R.A.V. v. City of St. Paul, 505 U.S. 377 (1992).

Rasul v. Bush, 542 U.S. 466 (2004).

Regina v. Dudley & Stevens, 14 Q.B.D. 273 (1884).

Rochin v. California, 342 U.S. 165, 172 (1952).

Rumsfeld v. Forum for Academic and International Rights, Inc. (FAIR), 126 S. Ct. 1297 (2006).

Talley v. California, 362 U.S. 60, 64–65 (1960).

Terminiello v. City of Chicago, 337 U.S. 1, 37 (1949).

United States v. Curtiss-Wright Export Corp., 299 U.S. 304, 317–22 (1936).

United States v. Miller, 425 U.S. 435 (1976).

United States v. Progressive, Inc., 467 F. Supp. 990 (W.D. Wis.), appeal dismissed, 610 F.2d 819 (7th Cir. 1979).

United States v. United States District Court, 407 U.S. 297 (1972).

United States v. Verdugo-Urquidez, 494 U.S. 259 (1990).

Virginia v. Black, 538 U.S. 343 (2003).

Youngstown Sheet & Tube Co. v. Sawyer, 343 U.S. 579 (1952).

Zadvydas v. Davis, 533 U.S. 678 (2001).

LEGISLATION AND TREATIES

Convention Against Torture and Other Cruel, Inhuman or Degrading Treatment or Punishment, 1465 U.N.T.S. 85 (1984).

Department of Defense. Military Commission Order No. 1: Procedures for Trials by Military Commissions of Certain Non–United States Citizens in the War Against Terrorism (March 21, 2002).

Espionage Act of 1917, 18 U.S.C. § 793.

Foreign Intelligence Surveillance Act, 50 U.S.C. §§ 801 *et seq.*

Official Secrets Act 1989, c. 6 (U.K.).

Posse Comitatus Act, 18 U.S.C. § 1385.

Stafford Act (Robert T. Stafford Disaster Assistance and Emergency Relief Act), 42 U.S.C. §§ 1521 *et seq.*

USA PATRIOT Act, § 215, 50 U.S.C. § 1861(a)(1).

Index

CPSIA information can be obtained at www.ICGtesting.com
Printed in the USA
LVOW10*1629161015

458580LV00009B/31/P